Racing Ironman W
Everything You Nee

MW00961607

Other Books by Raymond Britt

Qualifying for Kona: The Road to Ironman Triathlon World Championship

Epic Cycling: The Legendary Ironman Bike Course Guide

Racing Ironman: From Debut to Kona and Beyond

Ironman Lake Placid: Racing Strategies and Tips

Boston Marathon: The Legendary Course Guide

Chicago Marathon: Images of Sports

**Racing Ironman Wisconsin:
Everything You Need to Know**

By Raymond Britt

ISBN 1450529846
978-1450529846

10256007301018491000

1 2 3 4 5 6 7 8 9 10 9 8 7 6 5 4 3 2 1 1000

Published by RunTriMedia Publishing
Chicago IL, Scottsdale AZ, Boston MA

Printed in the United States of America
Visit us at www.RunTriMedia.com and www.RaymondBritt.com

For Wendy, Amanda, Rebecca, Eric and Kirsten

Contents

Acknowledgments

The world of endurance events is filled with generous people, communities, and institutions joining together in the spirit of swimming, biking, running, coaching, advising, writing, and more.

My participation in endurance racing, triathlon, and this book, have been inspired and driven by wide spectrum of people both on the course and off of it who joined me for the journey to the finish line and beyond.

My invaluable team of training, racing and supporting partners have included Steve Abbey, Art Hutchinson, Joe Foster, Michael McCormack, Barry Schliesmann, Kris Schriesheim, Rob Docherty, Kathy Winkler, Lisa Smith-Batchen, Michael Fisch, Marc Roy at SportStats Timing, Vinu Malik at xtri.com, Jesse Williams and Steve DeKoker at Brooks Sports, Adam Greene at Scott Bikes, Tim Moxey at Nuun, Rob Sleamaker at VasaTrainer, Jeff Banowetz at Competitor Magazine, and many more. I thank you one and all for the exceptional experiences we've shared so far.

My father traveled around the world with me to share many of the racing adventures included in this book, from Canada to Switzerland to Germany and ultimately to Hawaii. His love and support were everlasting, and I still feel his presence on the race course.

Wendy, Amanda, Rebecca, Eric and Kirsten have encouraged, inspired, shared and celebrated the journey with me from the beginning. This book is dedicated to them with unending love and thanks.

Author's Ironman Triathlon History

Race	Year	Swim	Tr1	Bike	Tr2	Run	Total
Vineman Ironman	1997	1:01:20	06:47	6:18:00	06:25	4:01:34	11:34:06
Ironman Canada	1997	1:14:55	06:30	6:15:55	05:20	4:05:01	11:47:40
Ironman Switzerland	1998	1:14:36	03:59	7:06:22	04:44	4:16:26	12:46:07
Ironman Europe	1998	1:12:08	04:33	6:17:36	04:04	4:02:10	11:40:31
Ironman Canada	1998	1:11:41	06:20	6:22:05	05:40	4:55:42	12:41:27
Ironman New Zealand	1999	1:11:32	07:45	6:23:00	06:40	4:19:07	12:08:04
Ironman Lake Placid	1999	1:19:15	08:28	6:34:49	03:05	4:17:04	12:22:38
Ironman Canada	1999	1:16:17	05:47	6:22:41	03:55	4:10:57	11:59:36
Ironman Florida	1999	1:18:43	06:43	5:35:01	02:52	4:12:38	11:15:57
Ironman California	2000	1:44:53	11:32	6:51:40	08:38	4:38:42	13:35:23
Ironman Florida	2000	1:17:01	06:55	5:44:39	03:21	3:57:46	11:09:40
Ironman Austria	2001	1:08:38	04:22	5:56:52	03:25	4:13:38	11:26:55
Ironman Florida	2001	1:10:35	05:33	5:35:07	02:18	3:46:42	10:40:13
Ironman Lake Placid	2002	1:10:46	05:31	5:41:37	02:13	3:33:46	10:33:51
Ironman Wisconsin	**2002**	**1:15:29**	**08:41**	**5:37:59**	**04:25**	**3:36:17**	**10:42:49**
Ironman Kona WC*	2002	1:18:57	04:01	6:01:54	02:15	3:50:14	11:17:21
Ironman New Zealand	2002	1:09:42	03:45	5:46:40	02:33	3:39:18	10:41:58
Ironman Lake Placid	2003	1:12:19	06:42	5:50:34	02:12	3:37:21	10:49:06
Ironman Wisconsin	**2003**	**1:08:54**	**06:00**	**5:32:10**	**02:07**	**3:48:47**	**10:38:24**
Ironman Kona WC*	2003	1:17:12	06:28	5:43:58	02:16	3:46:58	10:55:27
Ironman Lake Placid	2004	1:11:56	06:35	5:25:18	01:59	3:26:36	10:12:22
Ironman Wisconsin	**2004**	**1:09:38**	**06:00**	**5:25:08**	**02:10**	**4:09:37**	**10:52:30**
Ironman Kona WC*	2004	1:18:46	05:04	6:15:45	05:16	4:06:20	11:51:08
Ironman Arizona	2005	1:16:27	05:44	5:29:10	01:45	3:43:02	10:36:05
Ironman Lake Placid	2005	1:11:41	07:18	5:37:10	02:42	3:43:10	10:41:59
Ironman Wisconsin	**2005**	**1:14:12**	**06:51**	**5:42:08**	**02:09**	**4:33:33**	**11:38:51**
Ironman Arizona	2006	1:17:17	06:05	5:35:23	03:14	4:48:14	11:50:11
Ironman Lake Placid	2007	1:19:17	08:37	5:50:53	04:27	4:07:06	11:30:18
Ironman Wisconsin	**2007**	**1:28:37**	**10:09**	**5:54:36**	**05:26**	**4:14:08**	**11:52:55**

* Ironman Triathlon World Championship

Introduction

Each year, hundreds of athletes register for Ironman Wisconsin to compete in their first Ironman triathlon, or to race their first time on the Madison Wisconsin course.

I know what it's like to experience anticipation, curiosity and nervousness surrounding an Ironman triathlon. Prior to my first Ironman Canada in 1997, I devoured any information I could get about the race, the course, the conditions, and everything that seemed remotely relevant to completing an Ironman.

Candidly, I was afraid I might not finish the race. So I tried to leave nothing to chance. I figured if I did my homework, along with sufficient training, I would know what to expect on the course, and would be prepared to race it well.

As I prepared for Ironman Canada 1997, I made it a point to keep priorities in order. Family came first, and work was right behind. Triathlon was an exciting and challenging hobby, but it took a back seat to the important things in my life.

I'd expect the same is true for most of you reading this Book. Consequently, most of us don't have endless time to train and prepare for these events. We are not pros, we are not sponsored, we are given no breaks to train as much as we might think necessary to be completely prepared for our best Ironman triathlon race.

So we have to be smarter. We need to know everything about the race as possible. You want to know exactly what I did as I prepared for my first Ironman triathlons: what to expect, what the race is like, what can go right, what can go wrong, what it's like to deal with challenges on the course, what the course looks and feels like, etc.

Fast forward to ten years later after my first Ironman, and I've completed 29 Ironman triathlons overall. Five of them have been in Wisconsin.

Immediately after each Ironman Wisconsin finish, I wrote detailed reports about that year's race experience. Originally, my idea was to keep the notes for reference approximately one year later, when I prepared to race on the course again. The earlier notes helped me visualize the course, the experience, the conditions as I planned my race day.

Now that I've completed five Ironman Wisconsin races – 2002, 2003, 2004, 2005, and 2007 – and observed the 2006 and 2009 races as a photographer and reporter from the sidelines, I've accumulated the material contained in this

Book. Each race brought different performances, different conditions, different outcomes, and different lessons. During those years, I qualified for Kona twice, but also struggled to finish. I had excellent days, and difficult ones.

The experiences are all presented here.

The first chapter, <u>What to Expect on the Ironman Wisconsin Course</u>, was written prior to the 2007 race, about the overall course and race experience. It serves as a general race overview.

The next six chapters detail my experience and perspectives from each Ironman Wisconsin since the race's debut in 2002.

Chapter 2, <u>Ironman Wisconsin 2002: Debut in Madison</u>, describes my first race on the course, compares the course to the Ironman Lake Placid course (which I had finished seven weeks earlier), and includes strategy during the race to finish with a qualifying spot for the 2003 Ironman Triathlon World Championship in Kona Hawaii.

Chapter 3, <u>Ironman Wisconsin 2003: 100-degree Finish</u>, describes the hottest Ironman Wisconsin ever, what it was like to compete in the vigorous heat, while trying to earn a repeat visit to the Ironman Triathlon World Championship.

Chapter 4, <u>Ironman Wisconsin 2004: Down, But Not Out</u>, details what was my best Ironman race ever, until it all went bad deep into the run. It was my first stunning defeat on the course, but I was able to extract new lessons while finishing under 11 hours.

Chapter 5, <u>Ironman Wisconsin 2005: Finishing Against the Odds</u>, steps back to observe the overall race while still racing. I posed the question 'what drives you?' and examined the way others competed, what made them thrilled to become Ironmen and Ironwomen, and their emotions at the finish.

In Chapter 6, <u>Ironman Wisconsin 2006: Observations From the Sidelines</u>, I tell what it's like to watch an Ironman as a spectator. I had become a little burned out by Ironman racing in 2006, so I skipped the race. My son and I visited various spots of the course during the race, and saw some amazing athletes. It opened my eyes about Ironman races from a different point of view.

Chapter 7, <u>Ironman Wisconsin 2007: Rider's-Eye View Perspective</u>, is dedicated to breaking the bike course down, mile-by-mile in terms of elevation changes and speed from my actual 5:53:57 bike split during that race, and provides access to the complete archive of photos I shot from the bike.

The last chapter, <u>Everything You Need to Know to Finish an Ironman</u>, resulted from answers I've given hundreds of athletes over time regarding what to do before and during the race, relative to all the details. It assumes you've done the training, and focuses on everything else you might need to know, from nutrition to bike setup, from transition to finish.

Photos throughout this book were taken by me before, during and after various Ironman Wisconsin races in 2005, 2006, 2007 and 2009. I hope this Book provides you the information you need to have a great Ironman Wisconsin race. If there are some questions that still need answers, feel free to contact me via my website, <u>www.RunTri.com</u>.

The Destination

What to Expect at Ironman Wisconsin

Details, Entry, Schedule. Athletes, Kona Slots

What to Expect at Ironman Wisconsin

Since 2002, Ironman Wisconsin has been held in the welcoming college town of Madison Wisconsin on the second Sunday in September. Each year, more than 2,500 athletes converge on Madison to participate in this Ironman, which features a 2.4 mile swim in Lake Monona, a 112 mile bike ride through Wisconsin farmland, capped by a 26.2 mile marathon run through the University of Wisconsin campus to a finish line at the state capital building steps.

It's a tougher race than meets the eye. Weather conditions can fluctuate wildly. A seemingly tame bike course, based on comparing elevation changes with Ironman races in Lake Placid and Canada, can actually be as challenging. And if the heat reaches 90 degrees or more, as it has in the past, the marathon becomes a race of attrition.

I've completed the event five times, and observed it as a spectator once. So, having seen it from both sides, I can tell you just about everything you need to know to finish Ironman Wisconsin.

Before the Race

Registration tends to go smoothly in the Monona Terrace building, which serves as Race Central and the transition and bike rack areas on race day. Take a tour of the building; it's one of Frank Lloyd Wright's modern designs, with a terrific view of Lake Monona.

You can swim in Lake Monona in the days before the race, per the race schedule. Drive the bike course, of course, to check out the terrain. You will not be intimidated, as the elevation changes are slight. Don't be fooled.

The run course is not easily inspected before race day. It's on roads, closed streets, through a stadium and on a bike path. See what you can, and don't worry about it. It's not a terrifying run course. You'll see it on race day.

Bike and transition check-in occur on Saturday. You will rack your bike in perhaps the longest bike area you've seen in a triathlon, completely across the top Monona Terrace parking deck. You will place your bike and run transition bags in numerical order rows in two respective transition rooms inside Monona Terrace. Make a mental note of generally where the bags and your bike are; on race day it will be pretty easy to find them.

Make sure you put a tire/tube, CO_2 and appropriate bike tools on your bike. I saw too many people with flats or other problems, standing on the side of the Ironman Lake Placid course last month, waiting for the bike crew to come fix their bike. Sorry, it's not supposed to work that way; they're there for extreme situations. Be responsible; carry what you might need.

Overnight and race day conditions can vary widely, and past races have seen 39 degrees at 7am, cold pouring rain all day, or scorching heat. Consider having extra clothing in your transition bags: arm warmers and a vest in your bike bag for cold conditions. Put plastic bags over your bike seat and handlebars, to protect from overnight dampness or rain.

Then, eat well and get a good night's sleep.

Race Morning

The pre-race process is simple and smooth at Ironman Wisconsin. Body marking takes place on the northern, top deck of Monona Terrace. There tend to be more than enough people doing body marking, so the wait won't be too long.

After that, you are free to visit your bike to add nutrition, etc., and you can check your transition bags. Assuming everything is in order, venture inside the Monona Terrace building and find a spot on the floor for last minute relaxation and preparation.

Make sure you leave the transition area by about 6:20pm, and begin approaching the swim start area. Normally I would not counsel a departure this early, but the swim start entry area is quite small, and it always takes a long time to get more than 2000 swimmers through a narrow water's entrance (over the timing mats).

Complicating things a little is that there's almost no shallow area for swimmers to adjust to the water before swimming ahead. You have to go right in. But the athletes tend to pause before entering, dipping a toe in the water, so to speak, and everything backs up. Trust me, you need to allow extra time to enter the water.

Once in the water, unfortunately, you will have to tread water until the 7am start. Unlike the swim venues in Lake Placid or Canada, for instance, there is no beach on which to rest a little. You will be out in open water, using up a little energy. Try to relax and float on your back; it's not a bad way to pass the time before an Ironman race, appreciating the sky.

Swim

The Ironman Wisconsin swim is a two-loop, 2.4 mile swim in Lake Monona. The water tends to be flat, but I have noticed a small current that seems to be there every year. Nothing that will affect your swim start.

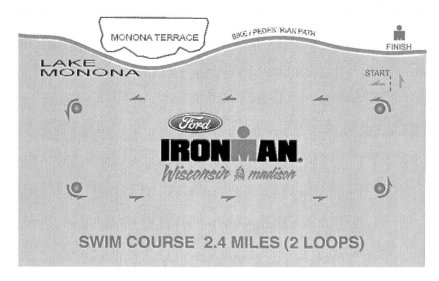

The starting line is quite wide, maybe 200 meters or so, split by a water-skiing jumping ramp. The ramp is a decent starting guide; if you want to start wide of the pack, stay to the right of the ramp. If you desire some physical contact in an attempt to go with the fast folks, be my guest: line up to the left. I usually stay to the right.

The mass start is still not without the usual Ironman swim commotion and messiness. The course heads south, with the rising sun in your eyes and the splashing of eager triathletes around you. Visibility will be compromised in the beginning, as it usually is. Just stay with the swimmers around you, and the first few hundred meters will speed by relatively quickly.

You'll then make one left at the first large orange cone, swim a couple hundred more meters, and take another left, to begin your northbound return to the starting area. This time, you'll be able to sight very easily, with the shore, the downtown Madison skyline and Monona Terrace in clear view.

However, it's on this northbound section that I have felt the tugging of slight currents in the past. Actually, I don't feel it, but it pulls me inside the buoys lining the route. I get too busy watching Monona Terrace pass that I fail to recognize that I'm being pulled off course to the left. After correcting a couple of times, I get better. But pay attention to the possibility; it creeps up on me each time.

Things will thin out somewhat on the second lap, and it's up to you to keep a steady pace, while also reserving most of your energy for the rest of the race day. Making the final turn on lap 2, you will spot the exit area, and be glad you're almost there. But even after you swim pass the starting line, you will still have a short distance to go. Be patient, you'll get there.

Once out of the water, you'll steal an anxious glance at the clock. Were you fast or slow? My advice: don't let the time on the clock elate or depress you too much. Times in the Lake Monona water have varied for me, and usually are a bad predictor of the kind of day ahead. Sometimes, the course is slow, sometimes it's fast. It is what it is, just head towards your bike.

Swim to Bike Transition

Steps after you're ashore, you'll be greeted by delightfully cheerful volunteers who are eager to remove your wetsuit for you. It's not mandatory, but can be fun, especially for first timers. Flop on your back, and they rip it off; hop up and run toward transition. Or run through all the fuss and remove your wetsuit in the changing area. I usually do the latter.

Getting to the transition changing area is most unique. It involves running from the first to the third floors of the parking structure on its circular ramp, referred to as 'the helix'. Spectators line the path, and you can run or walk up the helix. It takes time, but also allows your head to clear a little after the swim.

Run into the building, grab your swim-to-bike transition bag in one room, and keep moving to the changing area. Since about one person per second enters this area during peak time, there probably will be no chairs to sit on. Just find yourself a spot on the carpet, and change there. Helmet, bike shoes, gloves, bib number, sunglasses, and off you go, out the door to find your bike.

You will have to run some distance, to the far north of the parking deck to enter the bike area, then the complete length of the deck to the south exit area, while pausing to get your bike along the way.

You will not set speed records during this transition. It will take several minutes for you and for everybody. Don't panic, don't rush, just move smoothly. You'll do fine. Then down the south side helix, and you're onto the bike course.

Bike

The 112 mile Ironman Wisconsin bike course starts fun and fast, then gradually eats away at you over the miles. It throws no serious difficulty your way, but it refuses to yield over most of the course. Go out too fast, and you can suffer later.

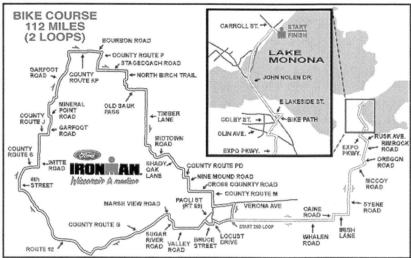

With that as a sort of warning, the first 16 or so miles, out to the two-loop section, are a good warm-up, taking riders to the west of Madison, from the small city toward classic Midwestern farmland. Some small rollers stretch your leg muscles, and a couple of pretty steep but short downhills will give you a speed boost, but also provide warning that they may hurt you a little on the way back.

Reaching the 39-mile loop section, you'll continue west on relatively tame terrain until you approach the town of Mt. Horeb. Approaching mile 30, you'll be faced with about a 1/2 mile long climb that veers to the left then right, where you'll be greeted by aid station volunteers. Get what you need, then prepare for five miles of work.

Miles 30 to 35 (and 70 to 75 on the return trip) take riders through relentless up-down riding that I like to call The Rollercoasters of Witte Road and Garfoot Road. Passing between and through farms, these miles toss it all at you: fast declines followed immediately by sharp uphills again and again, with short stretches of reasonably flat road connecting the little challenges.

At first, it's fun. Then getting over the next hill gets tougher each time. You'll think you're done, then there's more. You'll see when you get there. You don't want to be bonking the second time you ride this section. It's a bad place to be on the rocks.

Next up is a slightly dangerous fast, swerving downhill on northern Garfoot Road. You'll wish you can take it at full-speed, but only the most expert of riders can do it. It's too easy to lose control on the sharp turns here. Sacrifice a few seconds for better control.

The course flattens out on the top half, east-bound road for a few miles, allowing you to relax a little. You'll need the break, because when you make a right turn at Country Road KP to begin a southward path toward the start of loop two, the course's most challenging climbs await.

The climbs – at Old Sauk Pass and on Timber Lane – aren't very long, but they can be quite taxing. When you arrive there, settle into your easiest gear, sit back, and pedal as efficiently as you can.
Stay steady for the next few miles until you reach the town of Verona, where you'll be greeted by a cheering crowd that treats you as if you are a Tour de France rider. Savor the moments, smile at spectators and enjoy your short time there. Because after it's over, you are heading back to lap 2.

You'll finish lap 2 at about 95 miles, with 17 more to go. Depending on the heat, wind and your nutrition and hydration at that point, those last miles may be relatively breezy or can be very challenging.

Don't let the apparent downhill back to town on the race website course map fool you. It's more work that you'll expect. Be prepared mentally and physically at that point, and you'll do fine.

Run

The 26.2 Ironman Wisconsin marathon course is entirely self-contained in Madison's downtown and college campus area.

You will run two 13.1 laps, starting at Monona Terrace and immediately passing the State Capitol building. You'll descend past the capital on State Street before heading southwest on side streets approaching the Camp Randall football stadium. One of the small treats of this marathon course is running around the field on both laps; a unique experience.

Exiting the stadium, you'll then head north and west toward Lake Mendota, toward some welcome cool air and shade of the Temin bike path along Lake

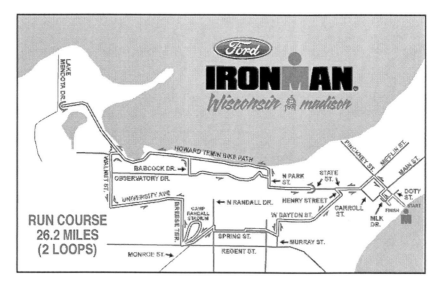

Mendota, heading east at first. You'll step off the path onto Observatory Drive, which brings you to the toughest climbs on the run course. My advice to most runners: unless you're gunning for a Kona slot and can't afford to sacrifice anything, walk up these hills. You'll lose a few seconds by powerwalking, but your legs will be most happy for the break.

After flying, sort of, down the other side of Observatory Hill, you'll enter the Party Zone of the run course, on State Street. You'll encounter the most spectators on the run course here, and they provide smiles and encouragement. Smile and nod in appreciation, if you can. Get to the turnaround, and your name and hometown will likely be announced to everyone there.

After the fun on State Street, you'll return to the westbound Temin Bike path. It's the longest uninterrupted stretch on the run course, and you won't be faulted for thinking the turnaround will never come. Stay with it, make sure to hydrate well at the several aid stations on this section, and keep moving forward. The good news is that after the turnaround, it's not a long return trip to town, maybe four miles.

On the way back, you'll head southeast toward Camp Randall then retrace your steps from there to the State Capitol. The finish line will be just meters in front of you as you make the turnaround to begin lap 2. It's not a fun moment for anyone, but just tell yourself as you head back onto the run course you're getting closer to the finish with every step.

After experiencing the first lap, you'll see there are no dramatic tests on the run course, and you'll be able to focus on moving steady and on getting the hydration and nutrition you need.

As the miles slowly pass, begin to think about your finish, and soon you'll be there. It's a kick to approach the State Capitol in the final few hundred meters, knowing that the finish line is just beyond it. And in a nice, but too-late gesture, the finish area is on a downhill slope.

Though you'll be tempted, don't use the force of gravity to sprint through the finish line. Take it slow and easy, and soak in those last few moments. You deserve it. So do the others around you. Don't blast past the guy in front of you and ruin his finish and finisher photo. Be polite and let everyone experience the finish they've been envisioning for months.

You've been envisioning it, too. You'll get there, and you will be declared an Ironman. Congratulations in advance.

etails, Schedule, Athletes, Kona Slots

Ironman Race Calendar

Ironman Wisconsin in the first race of the season that offers Kona qualifying slots for the following year's race in Hawaii.

Race	Kona Slots	Race Date
Ironman Malaysia	36	2/27/2010
Ironman New Zealand	75	3/6/2010
Ironman China	50	3/14/2010
Ironman Australia	60	3/28/2010
Ironman South Africa	30	4/25/2010
Ironman St. George	65	5/1/2010
Ironman Lanzarote	60	5/22/2010
Ironman Brazil	50	5/30/2010
Ironman Japan	50	6/13/2010
Ironman France	35	6/27/2010
Ironman Coeur d'Alene	65	6/27/2010
Ironman Germany	120	7/4/2010
Ironman Austria	50	7/4/2010
Ironman Switzerland	72	7/25/2010
Ironman Lake Placid	72	7/25/2010
Ironman Regensburg	50	8/1/2010
Ironman UK	30	8/1/2010
Ironman Louisville	72	8/29/2010
Ironman Canada	72	8/29/2010
Ironman Wisconsin*	72	9/12/2010
Ironman World Championship		10/9/2010
Ironman Florida*	72	11/6/2010
Ironman Arizona*	72	11/21/2010
Ironman Cozumel*	50	11/28/2010
Ironman Western Australia*	40	12/4/2010

* Slots for Kona 2011

Details

- **Race Date**: September 12, 2010
- **Location**: Madison, Wisconsin
- **Field size**: around 2700 registered
- **Kona Slots**: 72 (7 for pros, 65 for all others):
- **2.4 Mile Swim**: 2 laps in Lake Monona
- **112 Mile Bike:** 2 laps west to Verona
- **26.2 Marathon:** 2 laps though the city
- **Website**: www.ironmanwisconsin.com
- **Race Headquarters**: Monona Terrace
- **Notable Area Attractions**: Wisconsin State Capitol, University of Wisconsin-Madison, Frank Lloyd Wright's Monona Terrace
- **Weather**: averages tend to be 60s and generally sunny, but conditions have varies from cool rain to extreme heat in different years

Registration: Entry Fee $575

- All participants in the current year's event will have the opportunity to register on-site for the following year's event on the Saturday before the race.
- On-site general registration will open the morning after the event. Individuals may only register themselves; they will not be allowed to register a friend at any event.
- All remaining slots will open for registration online via Active.com at 12:00 p.m. local race site time the day after the current year's race.
- Please check the event website 2 months prior to the race, for more detailed information.

Note: race is typically sold out to general entry immediately; possibilities may exist to enter via the Community Fund; see www.ironmanusa.com

Anticipated Race Week Schedule

Day		Time	Activity
Thursday	9/9/10	7:00 AM	Gatorade Gear Check
		10:00 AM	Athlete Check-In
		10:00 AM	Ford Ironman Expo
Friday	9/10/10	7:00 AM	Gatorade Gear Check
		10:00 AM	Athlete Check-In
		10:00 AM	Ford Ironman Expo
		11:00 AM	Press Conference
		5:30 PM	Welcome Dinner
		7:30 PM	Mandatory Athlete Meeting
Saturday	9/11/10	7:00 AM	Gatorade Gear Check
		7:30 AM	Kids Fun Run Registration
		8:00 AM	Volunteer Team Information Meeting
		8:30 AM	Kids Fun Run
		9:00 AM	2011 On-Site Registration 2010 Athletes Only
		9:30 AM	Kids Celebration
		10:00 AM	Ford Ironman Expo
		10:00 AM	Mandatory Bike & Gear Bag Check-in
Sunday	9/12/10	4:00 AM	Shuttle Bus Service
		5:00 AM	Transition Zone; Bodymarking
		6:30 AM	Athletes must be at the swim start
		7:00 AM	Race Starts
		7:50 AM	First Swimmer out of the water; first bike start
		8:00 AM	Shuttle Bus to Verona Loop Service
		9:20 AM	Swim Course closes
		12:30 PM	First Bike Returns; First Runner Begins
		3:30 PM	Approx. Time of 1st Finisher
		4:00 PM	Race Day Massage
		6:00 PM	Bike & Gear Check-out Begins
Monday	9/13/10	8:00 AM	Post-Race Massage
		9:00 AM	2011 for 2010 volunteers and general public
		9:00 AM	2011 Kona Registration
		9:00 AM	View & Order Race Photos
		11:00 AM	2011 Kona Slot Rolldown
		11:30 AM	Ironman Awards Banquet
		5:30 PM	Volunteer Appreciation Party

Competitors by Division

In 2009, bib numbers were assigned to 2688 registered triathletes. On race day, 2397 athletes began the race. Of those, 2176 finished within the 17-hour time limit. The remaining 221 athletes were not able to reach the finish line (DNF = did not finish).

Division	Finished	DNF	Starters	Total %
M18-24	89	7	96	4%
M25-29	178	11	189	8%
M30-34	238	22	260	11%
M35-39	324	32	356	15%
M40-44	329	39	368	15%
M45-49	220	29	249	10%
M50-54	151	19	170	7%
M55-59	66	7	73	3%
M60-64	23	5	28	1%
M65-69	9	1	10	0%
M70-74	1	0	1	0%
MPRO	23	5	28	1%
W18-24	17	5	22	1%
W25-29	77	4	81	3%
W30-34	122	10	132	6%
W35-39	110	6	116	5%
W40-44	95	8	103	4%
W45-49	48	4	52	2%
W50-54	34	2	36	2%
W55-59	9	4	13	1%
W60-64	3	0	3	0%
W65-69	1	0	1	0%
WPRO	9	1	10	0%
Grand Total	2176	221	2397	100%

Average Splits and Finishing Times by Division

Wisconsin	Swim	Bike	Run	Finish
M18-24	1:17:49	6:16:02	5:11:30	13:00:19
M25-29	1:18:30	6:15:29	4:58:19	12:46:35
M30-34	1:17:37	6:14:04	5:00:46	12:46:57
M35-39	1:19:54	6:21:40	5:06:45	13:04:37
M40-44	1:20:19	6:20:16	5:05:40	13:01:50
M45-49	1:20:21	6:25:26	5:13:35	13:16:14
M50-54	1:25:19	6:36:37	5:23:35	13:44:23
M55-59	1:22:55	6:38:48	5:22:20	13:45:05
M60-64	1:37:39	7:17:12	5:48:48	15:05:20
M65-69	1:24:49	7:08:28	5:34:07	14:30:38
M70-74	1:28:01	8:10:00	6:31:37	16:31:10
M75-79				
MPRO	0:57:19	5:02:48	3:47:44	9:53:12
W18-24	1:24:29	6:55:03	5:18:48	13:56:04
W25-29	1:20:49	6:49:40	5:10:24	13:37:15
W30-34	1:21:37	6:58:08	5:14:06	13:50:39
W35-39	1:22:54	6:48:42	5:12:24	13:40:52
W40-44	1:23:42	6:53:05	5:23:44	13:57:50
W45-49	1:21:37	6:57:42	5:26:13	14:04:59
W50-54	1:27:27	7:07:15	5:34:03	14:27:48
W55-59	1:32:03	7:08:37	5:55:03	14:54:16
W60-64	1:41:58	7:30:13	6:11:34	15:37:40
W65-69	1:52:45	8:13:29	6:27:55	16:53:39
W75+				
WPRO	1:04:52	5:27:53	3:45:11	10:24:00
Grand Total	1:20:28	6:29:28	5:10:02	13:16:29

The average finish time at Ironman Wisconsin 2009 was 13:16:29. A key driver of the notably high finish time is the bike course difficulty. And the run course is even harder, compared to 21 other Ironman Courses. .

Toughest Ironman Course Ranking, Based on Average Finish Time

	Swim	Bike	Run	Total
St. George	1:21	7:02	5:07	13:47
Wisconsin	**1:20**	**6:29**	**5:10**	**13:16**
Malaysia	1:26	6:21	5:19	13:15
Cozumel	1:08	6:39	5:11	13:11
UK	1:24	6:53	4:34	13:10
Coeur d'Alene	1:20	6:27	5:05	13:08
Canada	1:17	6:23	5:08	13:00
Lanzarote	1:09	6:59	4:38	13:00
Lake Placid	1:16	6:34	4:47	12:54
South Africa	1:18	6:18	5:00	12:52
Louisville	1:23	6:21	4:48	12:51
Arizona	1:20	6:08	4:58	12:43
Florida	1:21	6:02	4:57	12:37
France	1:17	6:24	4:34	12:32
New Zealand	1:09	6:17	4:36	12:15
Australia	1:04	6:15	4:54	12:13
Brazil	1:20	6:03	4:40	11:59
W Australia	1:11	5:52	4:48	11:52
Austria	1:15	5:46	4:31	11:45
Germany	1:11	5:42	4:34	11:39
Kona	1:13	5:56	4:17	11:37
Switzerland	1:15	5:48	4:17	11:30

Yes, that's right. Wisconsin is the second toughest Ironman, according to this analysis. My experience on twelve different Ironman courses confirms that the ranking is well-earned.

Qualifying for Kona at Ironman Wisconsin

The Ironman Kona slot allocation protocol, as defined by
www.ironmanusa.com, is the following:

"At least one Kona slot shall be allocated IN FULL-DISTANCE EVENTS to
each five-year age-group category in which any age group athlete sends in an
application, both male and female, per the age group categories listed.

Be aware that some age groups may be combined for the allocation of a Kona
slot at the sole discretion of the race director. If there are no athletes entered in
the race in a particular age group, then that slot will be moved to the largest
populated age group in that same gender. For additional age group slots, slot
allocation shall be representative of the actual number of age group applicants
in each category in the race.

As an example, if 8% of the age-group applicants are females 40-44, then 8%
of these slots would be allocated in the female 40-44 category. Please note that
at 10 percent of Ford Ironman World Championship slots at full-distance
events are allocated to Pros, e.g,. of 80 qualifying spots, eight are reserved for
pros.

Note: All athletes must be present at Hawaii Registration to claim their spot."

Ironman Wisconsin offers 72 Kona slots, which were allocated in 2009 as
shown on the next chart. Generally, it's safe to assume that the slot allocation
will be somewhat similar in 2010. There may be movement of a slot or two
among divisions, such as adding a slot to M40-44 while subtracting one from
M18-24. But the allocation may change up until race day.

Kona Slots Allocated by Division by Race

Division	IM AZ	IM CA	IM CD	IM FL	IM LP	IM WI
M18-24	1	1	1	2	1	3
M25-29	3	3	4	3	3	4
M30-34	7	5	6	6	5	7
M35-39	10	8	8	8	8	9
M40-44	11	8	9	9	9	8
M45-49	7	7	7	7	8	6
M50-54	5	5	4	5	5	4
M55-59	2	3	2	2	3	2
M60-64	1	2	1	1	1	1
M65-69	1	1	1	1	1	1
M70-74	1		1	1	1	1
M75-79	1			1		
MPRO	6	5	4	5	4	4
W18-24	1	1	1	1	1	1
W25-29	2	2	3	2	2	3
W30-34	4	3	3	3	4	3
W35-39	4	4	4	4	3	4
W40-44	4	4	4	3	4	3
W45-49	3	3	3	3	3	2
W50-54	2	2	1	1	2	1
W55-59	1	1	1	1	1	1
W60-64	1	1	1	1		1
W75+		1				
WPRO	2	2	3	2	3	3
Grand Total	80	72	72	72	72	72

Very few slots per Division, it turns out. And the difficulty doesn't stop there.

Up to 2500 triathletes compete in Ironman Wisconsin. Things get tougher: in the highly popular Divisions, between ages 30-34, 35-39, 40-44, 45-49, and 50-54, for example, you'll need to finish among the top 3% or so of the group.

For the real Reality Check: look at the times turned in by the athletes that qualified for Kona in the 2008 Ironman Wisconsin race for Kona 2009.

Note: do not get discouraged when you see some extraordinary times posted by athletes in your age Division.

Don't let yourself be intimidated if you feel the gap between your current performance and ability and target qualifying times is too great.

You want to improve, you want to know the goals you're shooting for. If the goal is Kona – and it is if you're reading this – this is the starting point.

Most importantly, remember: every qualifying athlete listed on the following pages at one point could only dream of winning a Kona slot. Through hard and efficient training, they achieved the goal. With determination and perseverance, you will, too.

Kona Qualifying Times by Division

Ironman Wisconsin 2008 Qualifying Times						
Division	Swim	T1	Bike	T2	Run	Total
M18-24	1:00:21	5:24	5:04:31	2:28	3:02:29	9:15:12
M18-24	1:02:37	6:04	5:11:28	2:03	3:15:20	9:37:30
M18-24	1:03:16	5:10	5:23:39	1:40	3:13:08	9:46:51
M25-29	1:03:00	5:42	5:10:05	2:01	3:03:55	9:24:41
M25-29	1:09:31	4:56	5:13:32	3:02	3:03:31	9:34:30
M25-29	57:50:00	5:19	5:18:45	3:28	3:13:30	9:38:49
M25-29	59:03:00	5:35	5:15:23	3:47	3:15:46	9:39:32
M30-34	1:02:41	6:11	4:54:38	2:04	3:01:24	9:06:56
M30-34	1:02:03	5:31	5:05:22	2:25	3:17:23	9:32:43
M30-34	1:02:52	6:29	5:02:48	1:43	3:25:23	9:39:13
M30-34	1:02:54	5:52	5:28:59	1:51	3:00:43	9:40:19
M30-34	57:21:00	6:18	5:21:15	1:58	3:20:12	9:47:02
M30-34	57:19:00	6:18	5:21:52	4:17	3:18:14	9:47:59
M30-34	53:20:00	5:08	5:21:48	3:32	3:28:12	9:51:58
M35-39	1:02:08	6:43	5:03:36	2:28	3:05:12	9:20:05
M35-39	54:21:00	6:11	4:58:49	2:47	3:24:28	9:26:35
M35-39	52:25:00	5:33	5:18:20	1:36	3:25:47	9:43:39
M35-39	1:02:03	6:04	5:25:28	2:49	3:13:06	9:49:28
M35-39	1:06:43	6:36	5:14:00	3:29	3:18:50	9:49:36
M35-39	1:05:03	6:30	5:18:57	2:13	3:17:41	9:50:22
M35-39	1:01:12	6:47	5:21:01	2:42	3:18:58	9:50:38
M35-39	56:59:00	6:27	5:22:04	2:54	3:24:56	9:53:19
M35-39	54:33:00	5:25	5:20:13	1:54	3:32:19	9:54:22
M40-44	54:29:00	5:49	5:11:46	2:55	3:25:57	9:40:52
M40-44	58:44:00	5:50	5:18:17	2:15	3:16:38	9:41:42
M40-44	1:13:35	6:34	5:07:40	2:20	3:15:37	9:45:43
M40-44	57:26:00	4:59	5:14:19	2:31	3:32:28	9:51:40
M40-44	59:37:00	7:22	5:31:01	2:13	3:15:50	9:56:01
M40-44	1:01:12	6:09	5:11:54	3:29	3:33:41	9:56:23
M40-44	1:07:40	10:30	5:10:24	2:58	3:25:36	9:57:07
M40-44	1:10:44	7:25	5:18:12	3:05	3:23:44	10:03:08
M45-49	56:03:00	5:54	5:14:36	2:52	3:14:13	9:33:36
M45-49	1:07:52	7:57	5:13:45	2:29	3:41:03	10:13:05
M45-49	1:13:07	6:33	5:24:50	2:15	3:37:08	10:23:51
M45-49	1:11:47	6:54	5:31:10	3:53	3:39:28	10:33:11
M45-49	54:39:00	6:16	5:43:26	4:22	3:45:20	10:34:01
M45-49	1:07:53	7:51	5:26:54	8:23	3:45:17	10:36:17

Kona Qualifying Times by Division

Ironman Wisconsin 2008 Qualifying Times						
Division	Swim	T1	Bike	T2	Run	Total
M50-54	52:42:00	6:36	5:36:53	3:45	3:32:35	10:12:29
M50-54	1:00:40	7:49	5:32:51	2:32	3:32:56	10:16:46
M50-54	1:03:59	6:08	5:27:51	3:50	3:39:20	10:21:06
M50-54	1:14:31	7:07	5:16:11	2:55	3:54:25	10:35:06
M55-59	56:05:00	6:09	5:27:56	3:09	3:41:42	10:14:59
M55-59	1:07:56	6:40	5:43:01	3:40	4:04:45	11:06:00
M60-64	1:11:10	6:51	5:41:30	3:29	4:40:42	11:43:41
M65-69	1:24:23	13:58	6:14:48	7:46	4:35:59	12:36:52
M70-74	1:39:41	9:06	7:00:18	6:48	5:19:22	14:15:13
MPRO	51:52:00	4:26	4:48:41	1:53	2:56:40	8:43:29
MPRO	1:00:17	4:48	4:51:34	2:10	2:57:03	8:55:50
MPRO	55:21:00	4:08	5:04:31	2:08	2:53:34	8:59:39
MPRO	51:55:00	4:22	4:56:21	2:15	3:07:05	9:01:56
W18-24	57:48:00	6:48	5:49:33	3:39	3:49:44	10:47:29
W25-29	1:09:54	6:33	5:46:59	3:01	3:36:57	10:43:22
W25-29	58:41:00	6:47	6:12:10	3:50	3:54:33	11:15:59
W25-29	1:06:52	6:51	5:56:51	3:15	4:04:16	11:18:03
W30-34	1:04:15	5:42	5:48:19	2:55	3:32:28	10:33:37
W30-34	1:12:18	7:42	5:38:02	3:22	3:37:02	10:38:24
W30-34	54:21:00	6:27	6:00:07	3:50	3:48:25	10:53:09
W35-39	1:04:36	7:04	5:57:12	4:57	3:51:09	11:04:56
W35-39	1:10:22	8:06	6:05:20	3:13	3:38:16	11:05:17
W35-39	1:02:19	6:20	6:17:03	7:53	3:42:14	11:15:47
W35-39	1:18:23	9:06	5:56:54	2:42	3:55:49	11:22:52
W40-44	1:10:18	5:24	5:34:21	3:37	3:41:15	10:34:52
W40-44	1:01:54	5:58	5:57:13	2:48	3:41:57	10:49:49
W40-44	1:07:41	5:50	5:52:17	4:46	3:47:55	10:58:28
W45-49	1:08:56	6:27	5:51:59	3:27	3:33:53	10:44:41
W45-49	1:14:16	10:05	5:55:17	3:51	4:13:26	11:36:53
W50-54	1:05:26	8:16	6:11:26	4:26	4:16:23	11:45:56
W55-59	1:15:18	11:45	7:04:39	4:49	5:13:13	13:49:42
W60-64	1:08:54	11:40	7:05:24	4:53	5:55:38	14:26:28
WPRO	52:11:00	4:52	5:21:50	2:10	3:26:24	9:47:25
WPRO	1:04:33	5:37	5:13:01	2:14	3:24:23	9:49:46
WPRO	1:07:37	4:35	5:17:53	3:01	3:17:41	9:50:45

Racing Ironman Wisconsin

2002: Debut in Madison

2003: 100-degree Finish

2004: Down, But Not Out

2005: Against the Odds

2006: Observations From the Sidelines

Ironman Wisconsin 2002:
Debut in Madison

Immediately after the announcement of Ironman Wisconsin in the summer of 2001, I signed up to be part of the inaugural event, much as I had done three years earlier upon the announcement of the first Ironman USA in Lake Placid. I booked the race in my calendar, and went on my way trying to improve my Ironman performance at other races.

In November 2001, I finished Ironman Florida in 10:40, about 40 minutes from a Kona slot. Four months later in New Zealand, a 10:41 finish in wind and rain was about 20 minutes short of Kona. In July, it all came together in a 10:33 at Lake Placid, and my goal had been reached: Kona 2002.

I found myself at the Ironman Wisconsin start line at 7am on Sunday September 15 with an unexpected opportunity and challenge: qualify for Kona for the second time in seven weeks, this time for the 2003 race. I wasn't sure I was up to it.

In my pre race notes, I wrote:

" . . . frankly, after going all out in Lake Placid, and more recently at Mrs. T's, and just coming off an 8-day, very low training volume vacation, I wonder if my heart will be completely in it. The fire is returning, but will it be there September 15? Does it need to be?

"Worst case, it's a fun, long training day, close to home. Best case, though, it's a run at qualifying for Hawaii, 2003. This is the first qualifier for the 2003 race, which probably stacks the deck a bit against me. There are only 80 overall slots available, compared with 100 at Lake Placid, meaning that my age group might receive only 8 or 9 slots. Second, I assume I'll have to finish in the top 8 or 9 to get a slot; I anticipate no rolldown, since this is the first event of the year. Last, I will race hard, but, yes, I am mindful that Hawaii will be five weeks away, and will back off if and when necessary. "

Joe Foster, my Ironman training advisor, sensed my ambivalence, and let me have it two days before the race. To paraphrase, he said: 'if you're going to jeopardize a good performance five weeks later in Kona -- and you are by doing this race -- the pressure is on you to deliver; you've got a job to do; you need to qualify for Kona 2003, that must be your goal'.

It seemed a little harsh at the time. I tried to find ways to let myself off the hook, but I had to admit he was right: I had a job to do.

When I finished the race, the first question people asked me was: do you think you qualified? I didn't know. Second question: how does this race compare with Ironman USA Lake Placid? (which I had finished weeks earlier) That, I knew.

Both are great races, and I recommend each highly. I rate the courses as nearly equally challenging overall, but they are quite different in many obvious ways.

For starters, Ironman USA is set in the 1980 US Winter Olympic site of Lake Placid, a small town nestled in the Adirondack mountains, while Ironman Wisconsin is set in the heart of Wisconsin's state capitol, Madison, home of University of Wisconsin and its 40,000 students, surrounded by farming communities.

Madison, Wisconsin opened its arms and embraced this inaugural race in impressive fashion. The people were overwhelmingly friendly and supportive. The course wound through scenic farmland, through the university and with the state capitol building as the backdrop to the finish line. A photo-op race, if I've ever been in one.

The similarities begin and end with the swim. Both are two loop, rectangular courses in fresh water (although that term is less applicable to zero visibility Lake Monona than to Lake Placid's Mirror Lake).

Swim

At 7am in Madison, more than 1800 athletes took off to complete the two-rectangle loop swim in Lake Monona, in front of Monona Terrace convention hall, a unique structure inspired by Frank Lloyd Wright.

I expected a typical 1:10 swim, which I achieved in Lake Placid, but didn't get it in Madison.

The swim seemed more unpleasant than usual. I've never had so much contact in an Ironman swim. My favorite goggles developed a streaming leak after 400 meters. Some sort of current and/or my lousy navigating pulled me off course a few times. I kept running into people and having to stop and start again.

Approaching the clock at the end, I had no idea what it would read. But seeing 1:15:29, my heart sank. My worst swim in two years. Not a complete surprise, given the struggles in the water, but very disappointing.

Swim times were slower by several minutes for many racers. Of course I didn't know that until *after* the race, so for a while I was beating myself up for being such a lousy swimmer (actual thought: either quit triathlon or learn how to swim much, much better!).

I was smack in the middle of the pack, 873rd, compared to 792nd out of the water in Lake Placid. I thought I was out of Kona contention from the start. But I tried to remember Joe Foster's advice after a similar experience in Hawaii: never let the swim time distract you from the job at hand.

So off I went, to the most convoluted transition area in Ironman history. In Lake Placid, transition is fairly typical: run out of the water to the Olympic Speed Skating oval, to change and grab your bike and go.

In Madison, there was no such open area for a normal transition; instead the Monona Terrace building was the transition area. Picture this: run up four levels of a circular parking ramp (affectionately called 'the helix' by race officials) to the upper level parking garage, to the middle of the level, then inside (!) into a big Monona Terrace conference room to pick up your bag and to change. Then out the door, run fifty yards to bike entry, and scamper approximately a hundred yards to bike exit, which was a fun trip riding *down* the other side helix to ground level. It was amazing, and it took me and most people more than eight minutes to do it all.

After the transition area, in the first 1/4 mile of the bike on John Nolen Drive, there was a narrow path and a big bump I could not avoid. Bam! 4 PowerBars flew off my bike. No room to stop and fetch them, I kept going, with 920 fewer calories for the bike course than I needed.

All-in-all, not a good first 85 minutes in Madison. I wondered if it was my time for a 'bad day.' I had not fully recovered from Ironman USA, and I really didn't train for this race. I was so focused on Ironman USA, and had all training aimed at it, that when I was there, I wanted to explode. In Madison, it wasn't happening . . . yet.

Bike

I saw the Ironman Wisconsin bike course for the first time only the day before the race, and finally understood what people had been telling me for weeks: the course is unending turns and climbs. Some people who had trained on both courses had described the Madison course as harder than Lake Placid.

This surprised me, until I rode it. The elevation chart showed that these climbs took place within a range or 840 and 1240 feet above sea level, so no climb exceeded 400 feet at one time. That seemed reasonable, compared with 1500 foot climbs at Lake Placid. At least on paper.

But the difference between the two courses is simple: Lake Placid's climbs are long and arduous; Wisconsin's climbs hit you again and again.

Wisconsin's bike course is two loops, but the 40-mile loops began 16 miles from town. Lake Placid is two 56 mile loops. Winds seemed fairly strong out of the northwest in Madison, and were a constant test all day. But the sun remained out all day, unlike the downpour we got in Lake Placid.

Lake Placid's first seven miles are mainly up at 12mph, the next seven miles are straight down at 40+mph. A fairly flat few miles follow to the town of Jay, then riders work their way uphill back to Lake Placid. The most challenging aspect of the Lake Placid course is the 10-mile climb past Whiteface Mountain that begins at mile approximately 45 and 101. (More detail can be found in my Ironman USA xtri.com report.)

By contrast, the first leg of IM WI gently rolls along the countryside, getting you warmed up, and thankfully, there were no long climbs. Nothing seemed to exceed half a mile in duration. But they came one after the other, all day.

The Madison course runs mostly through Wisconsin's farmland, with just a few miles through local communities. Highlights were the extreme rollercoaster hills on Witte Road and beyond, passing through a cow path on North Birch trail to approach the toughest hill of the day, getting Gatorade from SuperWoman at the superhero aid station after mile 50/90, and blasting through crowds of people lining the road Tour de France-style, in Verona.

Passing through Verona at mile 55 was awesome, then we headed back west to begin the next 40 miles of the second loop. Through that point, I my confidence was building. I was riding fast, passing strong riders, and feeling more and more certain I could offset the poor swim if I kept up the pace.

By mile 60, though, I was beginning to feel noticeably sore and slow. I'm prepared for at least one bad portion on the bike; this was it. Doubts began creeping in again -- had I not recovered enough from Lake Placid? Would I recover in time for the hills on Witte Road and beyond? But you keep going, drink Gatorade, eat, and try to keep the cadence up. At mile 75, I felt myself again. Thank goodness.

The second loop finished, we headed back towards Madison, but not before a final climb to mile 105. The winds had picked up with more intensity, and speeds began to sag. At this point, I looked at my watch for the first time in more than 5 hours, and it said 6:40 had elapsed. After the slow swim, long T1, and a hilly course, I had a chance to arrive near the 7 hour point, not far off what I had done in Lake Placid.

I hammered back into town, and back up the helix to transition 2, as the clock read 7:02. I had finished the ride in 5:37:58, passing 607 riders, more than 1/3 of the field, to have the 157th best ride on the day. This was my best cycling rank ever, ahead of 244th in Lake Placid. Maybe I could salvage this race after all.

Run

The run course was filled with climbs, just like the bike course. I wasn't excited about it, but I knew it was more likely to tear down others, and I could use it to my advantage. As I exited transition 2 uphill towards the state Capitol, I knew if I were to have any chance at Kona, I'd have to make the run count.

The course elevation map shows 13 climbs of about 100 feet each, making this the most challenging Ironman run course I'd experienced. The Lake Placid course features two sharp hills at one and three miles into each run loop, the second of which was a long, half mile monster. But the rest of the Lake Placid course seemed flat.

In Madison, the run out of T2 goes directly uphill to the Capitol. After the capitol, the course heads out west through (nice touch!) Camp Randall, the Badger's football stadium, to an out-and-back on Observatory Drive through campus, and State Street, another out-and-back loop on the bike trail, then back to the capitol via the football stadium. I really liked this layout; always something different.

I had planned to check my watch to keep on pace, but I couldn't read it. I was too foggy. So I just ran as fast as I felt I could. My Kona hopes seemed diminished as I saw several in my age group returning to town as I was headed out, clearly far ahead.

I knew I needed to be top 10 in my age group (M40-44) to have any chance at a slot, and assumed there were many between me and the front-runners. But the beauty of the course is that you get four chances each look to scan who's ahead of you, at the turnarounds. Surprisingly, I didn't see that many in my age group. Was there a chance?

I reached the 13.1 mile turnaround at the Capitol, and looked closely at my watch for the first time since the run began. Not bad: 1:45 for 13.1 miles, and I felt fine.

I never had a bad moment on the run, perhaps because I kept eating. Having lost the Powerbars on the bike several hours earlier, I was concerned I'd run out of energy, so I took GU every 4 miles. I do this automatically in stand-alone marathons, but had never tried it in Ironman. It seemed to work.

I started recognizing people in my age group getting closer to me at the turnarounds, and passing the occasional one. Two things kept me on my toes: neighbor, training partner, and Iron rookie Barry Schliesmann was nearly exactly on my pace, about 4 minutes back, and #1338 also seemed to be eyeing me, trying to narrow the gap. They gave me a new motivation -- stay ahead. Each turnaround I checked, and each time they were still there.

I saw fewer and fewer male 40-44 runners on the last turnaround at mile 23, and started thinking -- without any real basis to do so -- that maybe I could go top 10. I had finished 13th in M40-44 at Lake Placid; maybe this could be a personal best ranking.

The key moment for me occurred on University Street, during mile 24. I spotted two M40-44 runners ahead of me, guys I knew were contenders. I knew they would not let me pass easily, being this close to the finish, and possibly close to a Kona slot.

I learned a lesson in Lake Placid, when I unsuccessfully tried to pass a final strong M40-44 runner near the end. I passed, he remained on my shoulder, and I couldn't shake him. When we were 50 yards from the finish, he pulled outside and outsprinted me to the finish. I couldn't answer.

In Madison, I didn't want to repeat this scenario. I needed to drop these two decisively, and waited until another runner passed them, hopefully distracting them, to make my move. I passed with as much sustained speed as possible, looked for shadows -- the sun was from the rear, and would outline anyone nearby -- and saw none. For the remaining two miles, I ran from the shadows (ultimately, I got three minutes ahead of them).

Running confidently, but on fumes -- I had no feeling in my hands or feet -- I passed the Capitol one final time, and headed for the finish. The clock showed 10:42:49 and 139th place and for the first time all day, I knew I had done well. I had passed 126 runners on the marathon.

I emerged from medical more than two hours later, in the dark, and returned to the finish line to see friend and training partner John Mueting finish his second Ironman with a smile. Then I looked on the results pages posted there, and saw what I had sensed: 10th place in my age group. My best Ironman age group rank at that point in time.

The next day, I collected my Kona 2003 slot.

Ironman Wisconsin 2003:
100-degree Finish

It had been fifty-one weeks since I qualified for the Ironman Triathlon World Championships in Kona. With Ironman Wisconsin as the first US Kona qualifier for 2004, I wondered if I could do it again. The fitness seemed there, but the track record wasn't quite where I had wanted it to be. Until recent weeks, my race season had been a solid one, but just not quite as good as 2002, and I hadn't had the breakthrough race that I was searching for. Ironman Wisconsin was the key race of the year, and I needed to hit it hard – this was the one that mattered.

As the final days approached, I typed out my vision for the race. I studied it. I internalized the message to the point that when someone would ask for my thoughts on the upcoming race, I'd find myself repeating sections of the typed text verbatim. The words were becoming the game plan for the breakthrough race I had been seeking.

Those words, written two days before the race, began with a sense of realism:

"This Sunday's Ironman is held in and around the university town of Madison Wisconsin. Last year I did not know what to expect, everything started badly, and I fought my way back to earn a Hawaii spot, somewhat to my surprise. This year, I am focused on qualifying for Kona 2004, but also aware that the field is more competitive and it will be a harder task. There are only 9 Kona slots available for the more than 280 competitors in my age group."

While my racing season had been pretty good, 2002 had been better, at least until August. Only my 6th place M40-44 at the Chicago Triathlon two weeks earlier had exceeded 2002 performance. And training levels seemed to be better in August. So the trend was good, but could it carry through to Wisconsin?

Swim

My pre-race words were less than optimistic about the swim, in an effort to prevent the temporary depression that typically sets in after a middle-of-the-pack swim result.

The 2.4 mile swim is a two rectangle loop in Lake Monona, and was terrible for me last year. It was messy, my goggles leaked and fogged up, I went off course, and I exited the water five minutes slower than at Lake Placid. I was supremely unhappy with myself, and that's not a good way to start a 10.5+ hour day. I hope not to repeat the scenario this year, but the swim is my least predictable event. If I can go 1:12:xx as in Lake Placid, I'll be pleased.

At 6:55am, I joined 1810 other athletes in Lake Monona and positioned myself near the front of the pack, but wide right from the crowd. The cannon urged everyone forward at 7:00am, and we were off. This was it . . . time to make things happen! Within the first sixty seconds, in the middle of the congested, churning, frothy water, my heart sank as water began streaming into my goggles. Last year's frustrating swim flashed in front of my eyes, with memories of having to empty my goggles every hundred meters or so. Was it going to happen again?

From the start, it appeared so. I was forced to pull up three times in the first few hundred meters to empty water and try to get a tight seal. Negative thoughts began creeping in, and I quickly searched for something positive: what could possibly be good about this little challenge? Answer: decide that a little running water in the goggles keeps the fog off the lens; hey! I can see the next buoy better! No more going off course! Repeat after me: Stay Positive.

As things began to clear up, I was able to better relax and concentrate on decent form. I was reaching and extending, and it worked. I was also very aware of swimming more efficiently on my side and flowing. Buoy after buoy passed by at what seemed like a good pace. As I swam the northward leg for the final time, catching glances of the Monona Terrace building brimming with spectators at a distance on my left, I began wondering what my swim time might be.

Approaching the swim finish, I felt fast, but I've felt fast before and seen 1:15:xx and hated myself (not really, but you get my point). Squinting at the clock a few meters away, at first all I saw was the 1 and the 8, and honestly thought: it could either be 1:18 or 1:08 and I wouldn't be shocked. What did it say?

When I reached the clock, it said I had reason to be happy: 1:08:54, my second best swim ever, and only 14 seconds short of a personal best. This put me in nearly the top third of racers, 673rd out of 1810 participants. A terrific way to start.

The swim-to-bike transition is the longest and most bizarre in triathlon, going from the beach up a four-story parking garage helix to a top floor transition area inside the Frank Lloyd Wright-designed Monona Terrace building. Then a run of about 150 yards across the whole parking lot to the other side to start the bike. Expect 0:08:30 for transition, hopefully onto the bike course as the clock reads 1:21:xx. If it's slower, it's beyond my control, and I'll have 9+ hours to gain time back.

Highly motivated by an unexpectedly good swim time, I sped through transition hoping to knock a minute or two minutes from last years' T1 time of 0:08:31. The process was a blur, but I do remember entering the bike course with the elapsed time clock reading 1:15:something, about six minutes ahead of my plan. In fact, my transition time was 0:06:28, nearly two minutes better than last year.

Bike

With this great start, I felt in perfect position to execute my bike pre-race bike vision:

"I want to explode on the bike course ('explode' being a relative term, given the distance and the need to preserve for the run), and I would like to shave several minutes compared to last year. I would be thrilled to come in somewhere between 5:28:xx and 5:33:xx, better than 20mph. I will have a carrot to chase; my local training partner — who's very close to me in terms of ability — will probably exit the water about 6-7 minutes before me, and I'll benefit by trying to catch him on the bike (and he'll benefit by trying to stay ahead!)."

I took off in search of speed and my training partner, Barry Schliesmann. In no time, I was flying out of town on John Nolen Drive, picking off riders one by one. The bike course consisted of approximately 17 miles out to a two-loop 39 mile route through beautiful farmland and supportive towns, before retracing the 17 miles back to Monona Terrace. As I passed markers every five miles, I could see I was riding well. I reached 20 miles in 54 minutes, or 22mph. This was great, but I knew the wind and the upcoming hills would bring that speed back to reality. Four miles later, I caught Barry, impossibly early. It turned out we had similar swims, and he had entered the bike course less than two minutes ahead of me. He was also a little tired; he had reason to be.

Barry had delivered a 10:21 at Ironman Canada two weeks earlier. He had also missed his Kona goal by 6 seconds, as he was blocked by a family going through the finish chute, and could only watch helplessly as he was passed by a runner who shot through the family to ultimately take that last slot. The 6-second miss capped a frustratingly star-crossed race season for him, and he was back at Ironman Wisconsin on a mission for Kona 2004. I thought something great was possible for him.

Tired or not, Barry stuck with me, and we soon settled into a well-known scenario. We had done long non-drafting training rides all season, trading the lead every two miles or so. This was the first time we got to try it in a race, and it was great. We flew through the town of Mt. Horeb, roughly mile 30 on the west side of the course, and cruised through the next five miles of roller coaster hills, including the triple threat rollers on Witte Road, still averaging 21.6 mph.

Reaching the north end of the course at mile 40 after some fast descents on Garfoot Road, I felt ok, but I was beginning to have trouble. My right iliotibial band had unexpectedly been tightening up, and would not let go. By mile 45, riding on a narrow road through a farmer's property on Birch Trail, a guy at the side of the road was counting off '. . . 207 . . . 208 . . .' as we rode past. It didn't take long to figure out that he was counting places, and that's where we stood in the race. It seemed like excellent positioning to me, and it kept my mind off the ITB pain as we ascended past encouraging costumed cheerleaders and taunting devils on the longest climb of the course: Old Sauk Pass. Two more steep climbs stood in our way before we steered into the excitement of Verona.

The town of Verona throws a huge party on Ironman Sunday, and between trips to the barbecue pit, people lined the town's main street to cheer riders in a Tour de France-like party atmosphere. Hundreds of screaming people, photographers and TV crews greeted us as we reached mile 56, halfway home. It should be an uplifting point in the race, and it was, briefly, for me. Unfortunately, I was rapidly feeling the first signs of an approaching bonk, signs that my race was beginning to fall apart way too early.

I had unintentionally not taken in enough Gatorade early on, and I was beginning to pay the price. Before the race, I decided to use only one bottle cage, to be more streamlined, assuming I'd reload at aid stations every 10 miles. The first aid station was 17 miles from the start, so I got behind because I had expected one earlier. Then I foolishly skipped taking a bottle at the 2nd and 4th aid stations because I hadn't completely finished the bottle I was carrying, and I was feeling good. I reasoned that I didn't want to be carrying extra weight, even in liquid form. Foolish rookie mistake by this veteran; saving a few ounces of weight was having too high a cost.

Shortly after Verona, the dehydration began to hit hard. I was feeling sore much earlier than usual and really getting thirsty. Staring at my empty Gatorade bottle, in a panic, I realized I had many miles to go to get to the next aid station, at mile 70 in Mt. Horeb. I tried to stay near Barry, but he slipped out of sight for good while I was fading and trying to control the damage. As the sun rose and the temperatures climbed into the 80s, I felt like I was drying up in the desert. Everything had been going perfectly. How could I have let this happen?

Sometimes I wish there was a flight data recorder to capture all the feelings, emotions and thoughts that occur during the Ironman bike ride, especially during the bad moments. The mind scrambles in a million directions as the body approaches Apollo 13 territory: there's been an explosion, now the question is — how to get back to earth in one piece from here? How do I not only survive the next few miles, but how can to put it back together to support the rest of the race? During some of these worst moments, I tried to find positive things to keep me going: images of friends made me smile; music constantly ran through my head, I was trying to absorb positive energy from the people, the action, and the sights and sounds around me. Dealing with these moments can be brutal, but they are also defining.

As I finally approached the next aid station in Mt. Horeb at mile 70, a rider passed me and asked how I was doing. I told him honestly: I'm bonking. He sneered back with words to the effect of 'you're not going to make it,' and sped by as if I was history. It made me mad, which was a good thing. It gave me the jolt I needed; I knew I'd prove him wrong, and noted his number. I was going to blow this guy off the course by the time the day was done. Just not at that minute; I needed to down 48 ounces of fluid, fast, and here was the aid station I had been hazily dreaming about for the last 30 minutes.

Aid station by aid station, I slowly pulled myself out of the deepest bonk I'd ever experienced on a bike course. I overcompensated — I took two 24 oz bottles at every station, and tried to force myself back to normal. I staggered through the rollers, the steep Old Sauk Road climb, and the two others, and it was coming back, but not fast enough. I normally take pain reliever and salt tablets at mile 100, but I gave in and took them at mile 90. Good move. All of a sudden, I started feeling better, and by the time I reached Verona for the second and last time, at mile 90, I was riding out of the saddle and thinking about making up time.

There's nothing like passing the mile 100 marker on an Ironman bike course, and feeling strong. After 40 miles dragging myself out of the hell of dehydration, there I was, heading back toward Madison, picking up speed again. The old me was back, passing rider after rider. The guy who sneered at me? I caught him at mile 105, and left him in my dust. Take that!

In the last miles on the bike course, I checked the readings on my bike computer, and they looked great. My speeds were coming back up, and it looked like I was going to have the ride of my life after all. All the long training rides, the speed of my new Softride Rocket, and the vision I had outlined before the race were coming together. As I had hoped before the race, I did in fact explode on the bike. It's just that I didn't intend it quite so literally, the good with the bad. Pulling up the four-story helix to enter the second transition, I had done what I set out to do: at 5:32:10, I had shaved several minutes off my 2002 Wisconsin bike split, and had delivered my fastest Ironman bike ride ever.

When done with the bike, back up the four story helix, change to running shoes, and out onto the two-loop 26.2 mile run course through the hilly state capitol and university areas. Because of the long transition zone, expect a 0:04:00 T2.

With the 112th fastest bike ride on the day, I had passed 466 riders, and when I handed my bike to a transition volunteer I was in 172nd place overall. Buoyed by this success, I sped through the second transition as fast as I could. I changed into the same Brooks Trance running shoes that had carried me to a 3:37 marathon at rain-soaked Ironman USA in Lake Placid a month earlier, put my Met-Rx hat on, and ran out the door having spent only 2:07 in transition.

Run

As happy as I was entering the run course for the first time ever with less than seven hours elapsed in an Ironman, I knew one thing: everything that had happened to this point suddenly didn't matter. It all comes down to how fast you can run the marathon. And I wanted to run a fast one.

I want to run my fastest Ironman marathon and that means I need to run faster than 3:33. I was too foggy to read the pace on my watch last year, but I need to pay close attention to times each mile. I need to average 8 minutes per mile to run a 3:30:xx. I think this will require pushing harder than I ever have before, so I hope I'm feeling decent when the time comes.

I had to admit I was feeling better than earlier in the day, but not as good as when I ran that 3:33 in Lake Placid 2002. Just shy of 2:00pm, I entered the run course with the temperature above 90 degrees, knowing that the next words I wrote before the race couldn't have been more on target:

"At this point in the race everything's up in the air, and it takes a perfect balance of previous effort, conservation, nutrition, hydration and conditions for a perfect run. All I can say is I will be going as hard as I can, and the clock will read whatever it reads at the end. The point of the journey is not to arrive; anything can happen."

I knew that I had not maintained that perfect balance and that a perfect run would, in fact, require pushing harder than ever before. This was going to be interesting.

The two-loop Ironman Wisconsin run course is unique in that it circulates through the center of Madison and its university, while other courses tend to mainly lie out of the main town. I had intended to run fast, and the first few miles went much better than the 8 minute pace I had wanted. My first mile, to and away from the Capitol was my fastest in an Ironman marathon: 6:41. Too fast. I eased back on the second, taking my first pit stop all day, and clocking a 7:56 on Spring Street, heading towards the football stadium. At this point, I finally caught up with Barry, who had entered the run course a couple minutes ahead of me. I passed him quickly but had the sense that he would hold on for a solid finish.

The next two miles to Observatory Drive were at 7:33 pace, and I began to wonder how fast this run might be. The combination of impending soreness and the steepest climb of the day led me to walk part of mile 5, and it came in at 9:24. But I got back on track with the next two miles, running 8:03 miles past wonderfully supportive spectators on State Street, and onto the shaded lakefront bike path.

But as soon as we approached blazing sun in an open field, the gears began grinding as hunger and dehydration became problems again. Mile 8 was an 8:22, and I knew I was slipping fast. At mile 9 on Walnut Street, both quads seized threateningly, and I knew if they didn't get better, I was in trouble again. Feeling like I was now running in quicksand, I began ignoring my watch, and focused on simply trying to save my run.

I had been carefully taking in at least a cup of Gatorade and a cup of Cola at aid stations every mile on the run, but it wasn't enough. There were probably also lingering effects from the bike bonk that were coming back to bite me. I began shuffling from aid station to aid station, downing a nausea-inducing combination — Gatorade, Cola, Water, GU gels, and where possible, chicken soup. At mile 11, I drank three cups of the soup to try to rebuild my sodium levels. The wheels were coming off my marathon, and I was hoping that something in that blend would help.

I moved on — I hesitate to call it running at that point because I don't think I was going very fast. But I did notice something important: no one had passed me, and I seemed to still be moving faster than others. I returned to the Capitol, registering a 1:50 half marathon time but I didn't even notice. I was just adhering to the last part of the pre-race plan: "I will be going as hard as I can, and the clock with read whatever it reads at the end."

As the intensity of the heat increased, and more people around me stopped running altogether, I remembered that in similar conditions at June's Ironman Idaho, 230 out of 1574 participants were unable to finish the course. Barry had raced there, too, and his 4 hour marathon was 100th fastest overall. So I had the feeling that even though I was going slower than hoped, it was due to conditions, and I had the very real chance of placing well in the marathon.

Miles 14 to 19 were a complete blur of tunnel vision to me, except for the wonderful spectators calling out support. There were apparently many xtri.com readers out there and I really appreciated the shouts of encouragement all day. They helped me come back to reality and I finally glanced at my watch again with 9:20 elapsed in the race, and about seven miles to go. For some reason, at that moment, a spark ignited the fuse. It was as if I had been given a new battery. I lit up inside, and said to myself: 'now or never, time to Lean Into It.'

The next seven miles were going to determine if I was going to earn a spot to Kona 2004 in this race. Last year at this same point, I had the distinct feeling, with no real reason, that I could get 10th in my age group. This year, I also had a distinct feeling, but it was about overall placing. I was feeling like 80th overall was possible, compared to 139th overall in 2002. I didn't really see that many people ahead, and no one had yet passed me. Well, one person did speed by me at mile 17, but ten minutes later he had passed out at the side of the road, and I never saw him again.

The final three miles of Ironman Wisconsin were slightly but painfully uphill, culminating in a short but steep climb to the Capitol. As I approached the last few hundred meters, I spotted and tried to pass what seemed like an endless number of runners. Unsure of who was on their first or second lap, as much as it hurt, I had to try to pass each one. Coming to the final right hand turn onto MLK Drive, and seeing the finish 100 meters away, I remembered Barry's 6-second near miss in Canada two weeks earlier, and couldn't take any chances. I broke into a full-on sprint for the finish, and charged over the line in 10:38:24.

I had no idea at the time, but I had just completed the breakthrough run of 2003 that I had been seeking. I had run the 57th fastest marathon overall, and had finished in 62nd place overall, by far my best Ironman finish ever. The best part: 6th place M40-44, and Kona 2004 Qualification. Icing on the cake: twenty-two minutes later, my training partner Barry Schliesmann crossed the line, and realized his Kona dream, too.

Ironman Wisconsin 2004:
Down, But Not Out

"How many of these things have you done?" a friend asked as I prepared to travel to the 2004 Ironman Wisconsin. I've done many Ironman triathlons, more than most, but I was reluctant to say the number (21). Because the point isn't the number. Instead, the point is that no matter how many Ironman races any of us have done, each time you venture onto an Ironman course, you're likely to experience something completely new, something that will further define your character. And in my 22nd Ironman, in Madison Wisconsin, this was indeed the case again. But in a way I never would have imagined.

I was returning to a course that had treated me well in 2002 and 2003. In both years, I had finished Ironman Wisconsin fast enough to earn Kona qualifying slots in the M40-44 age group. I was also coming off a personal best Ironman in Lake Placid, 10:12:22, just a few weeks earlier. I felt at or near my triathlon peak, and expected a great day as the sun rose over Madison Wisconsin on September 12, 2004.

Swim

The Ironman Wisconsin swim course is two loops in Madison's Lake Monona, and this year, the sun rising from the east made for a picture-perfect start. But it was a crowded picture. With the last of 2,188 racers scampering into the water just seconds before the cannon signaled the start, Ironman Wisconsin offered the most congested swim I've ever been part of. And while this staggering number of swimmers meant that most of us would be attempting to swim a straight line, to not run into too many others, and to get clobbered as little as possible, even that wasn't my biggest concern.

Two weeks earlier, I had encountered the completely unexpected, an asthma attack in the first 100 meters of the swim in Monroe Harbor at Chicago Olympic Distance Triathlon. I was stunned to find myself swimming to the side, gasping for air, just seconds after the race had begun. I hadn't pulled off a race course like this since my quite awful triathlon debut, in this same water and in this same race, exactly nine years earlier. What was happening?

I have active asthma, and while I had never knowingly experienced and asthma attack in a race, I have learned to carry an inhaler on the entire course, even in the water. I pulled it out of my wetsuit, took a couple of puffs, and tried to swim again. Not much better at first, and I again found myself grasping the harbor's edge again to catch my breath. 'This is silly', I thought; 'I should climb out and quit. Life's too short, and this seems dangerous.'

But I there was no ladder in sight, I had never quit a triathlon before, so I convinced myself to keep going. Eventually, I came around, and ultimately had among the top bike and run splits on the day. Even after losing a couple of minutes hanging on the side early on, I finished 8th in the M40-44 age group, about 90 seconds out of 2nd place. Not bad, I decided. At least this was only a tune-up race, no Kona slot on the line.

But I didn't want a repeat occurrence. So as I began the 2004 Ironman Wisconsin, I was determined not to push to the point of risking a similar episode on the swim. I just wanted to get out of the water in decent shape to begin my real race – on the bike and on the run.

After the start, on the occasions I was actually swimming and not avoiding others or being pulled on, I found myself thinking: I'm having a pretty decent swim. But as had been the case the previous two years, as I rounded the final turn and headed for the swim exit, I had no idea what my swim time might be. I had the same thought as in previous years: please let the clock have the second number on the clock be a zero and not a one! This time, my wish was granted: 1:09:32. Great. Now that's over, time to have some fun on the bike!

But first, there's a time-eating transition that is unmatched in triathlon. Run to the Monona Terrace parking ramp, scurry up four levels, enter the Monona Terrace building, grab your bike bag out of one conference room, enter another conference room to change, run out of the building and the entire length of about a 200 meter parking lot with your bike to the transition exit. In 2002, I accomplished this in about 8.5 minutes. I raced it this time, getting through all that in 6 minutes flat. I had hoped to get onto the bike course with less than 1:20:00 elapsed on the race clock; mission accomplished. With more than four minutes to spare. A good start.

Bike

After recording a personal best 5:25:18 bike split in Lake Placid this year, I was eager to try to beat that in Madison. Even though I'd raced Ironman Wisconsin twice before, I made the same mistake most people do when they consider the Madison-area bike course: we think, sure, a few hills, but nothing as steep as (fill in the blank – Richter Pass in Canada, last 10 miles back into Lake Placid, the road to Hawi in Kona).

Just one drive to view the course jolts you back to reality – this is a hard bike course. It's not the elevation gains; true they seem far less than others on a side-by-side comparison. It's the constant, unrelenting up/down that just chip away at you. Riding the course on Computrainer, based on GPS elevation coordinates, you see the data right in front of you: 4%, 5%, 6% humps, hills, climbs, over and over. Not for extended stretches, but just enough to rob your momentum and speed each time. But as you roll four stories down the parking ramp from the Monona Terrace transition area onto John Nolen Parkway, none of that matters. All that matters is riding your best, taking the challenges as they come.

Someone did the math, and determined that with nearly 2200 riders strung out on the course in non-drafting formation, they would stretch about 9 miles. I was #623 out of the water, so about 25% of the field was on the bike course ahead of me, with a few hundred of them within 10 minutes or so. And in the first few miles, things were backed up with long lines of riders. But I've learned to just stay left, announce my passing when necessary, until there's free space on the course. And that free space began opening up as we headed west into pure dairyland territory, with the scents that tell you you're in the heart of farmland.

The Ironman Wisconsin bike course is made up of a roughly 16 mile trip south then west to a 40-mile loop that is covered twice, followed by a return to town with a reverse commute on that initial 16-mile leg. The course, as mentioned above, is continuously hilly, but really taxes you heading north out of Mount Horeb from miles 30 to 35 (also 70 to 75 on the second leg), and a couple of challenging ascents at mile 45, and I'd guess mile 48 (also 90 and 93). The course is also almost entirely exposed, and with the sun rising on a warm and perfect day, the wind was kicking up from the south.

Having survived the swim without incident, I intended to do the same on the bike. In 2003, my unexpected problem was bonking badly on the bike due to poor hydration management (I didn't drink enough), and suffering from miles 55 to 90. I was determined not to make the same mistake twice, and stayed on top of hydration (a bottle every aid station) and nutrition (a GU every 10 miles; a PowerBar every 25 miles; bananas from aid stations).

I could feel the difference throughout the course. I kept arriving at spots where I remembered struggling in 2003 – the climb to Mount Horeb, the hills on Witte Road, Garfoot Road, and Old Sauk Pass – and found myself passing through them feeling fresh and strong. This was exactly how I had envisioned it. I was loosely aware of my pace, but was not using the watch or bike computer. I was riding on feel, and everything felt great.

I had mapped out a plan prior to the race that had a 5:25 bike split. Riding on feel for 112 miles – not gunning it or holding back – remarkably, I pulled my bike into the second transition in 5:25:08. A new PR over my Lake Placid ride, albeit by only 10 seconds.

I afforded myself only a fraction of a second to smile about this, as I raced through transition, entering the run course with 6:42:56 elapsed on the race clock. I was beginning the marathon more than three minutes earlier than I ever had in an Ironman race. Everything was going perfectly. All I had to do now was run a great marathon.

Run

I had run a great marathon in Lake Placid in July. Great for me, at least: 3:26:36. My marathons in Madison had been 3:36:17 in 2002, and 3:48:47 in the extreme heat of the 2003 race. Starting the run on PR pace, and doing some math based on those times, I knew Kona was within reach again.

The Madison marathon course is unique in that it remains within the town. The upside is spectator access; the downside is many twists and turns. The course zigs and zags. It has also changed somewhat in each of the three years Madison has hosted the Ironman. So for the first few miles, I wasn't really sure where we were heading. I just followed the arrows right, left, onto the pedestrian overpass, etc, until we reached familiar territory: State Street at mile 6, and the subsequent next three miles on a lakefront bike path.

Throughout the first lap, I ran steadily, passing people with some regularity, and noticing that there were not many ahead of me at the turnarounds. I reached the end of lap having run 1:44:58, more than 8 minutes behind my Lake Placid pace. Not great, but still one minute ahead of my 2002 marathon pace in Wisconsin. I just needed to keep it up. 13.1 more miles to Kona.

I headed past the Capital building on mile 14, back into the second part of the run course. By this time, I was not feeling well, but then I rarely feel great during miles 13 to 20 of any Ironman marathon. I remembered how bad it got in 2003, when I felt like I was running through quicksand as we headed toward the Camp Randall Football stadium. I reminded myself that I kept moving forward through these bad patches time after time after time. So I kept moving.

Then it all went bad in a way it never has before.

In a matter of a few minutes, I was audibly gasping for air, it all went blurry, and it all began to shut down. Shades of the Chicago triathlon two weeks earlier, but I decided the risk was less because I was not face down in water. 'Keep going', I told myself. 'You always get through these, run through it, keep going!' So I kept running, hoping to pull it out, but as the moments passed it seemed increasingly dangerous.

Then suddenly, full with the knowledge of how well I was doing, how close to Kona I might have been, I knew I was going down and there was nothing I could do about it. On autopilot, my body wrenched itself to the left side of West Dayton just short of the 15 mile marker. The next thing I knew, I was on my back under a tree, eyes closed but feeling like they were in the back of my head, surrounded by voices.

I could not move. I didn't want to open my eyes. I was just trying to breathe. It didn't dawn on me that the race was continuing without me. I had not idea what had happened, or what would happen next. I just lay there.

I heard a siren approach, and thought in a daze: 'I wonder who's having trouble?' It didn't register that it was for me, I was that detached. 'He's got an inhaler in his hand' one voice said to another. I don't remember how it got there. 'Do you have asthma?' I nodded. 'Air is bad here this week,' said the second voice. 'We've had fifteen racers pulled with asthma already. If I treat you, you'll be disqualified, do you understand?'

DNF . . .?

I understood, and had completely mixed feelings. Part of me had already decided that this had gone too far, it was too risky, that I needed help. The same part reminded me that I promised my wife after the swim incident in Chicago that I would not do anything stupid, and it seemed that continuing might violate that promise. That part of me had no qualms about pulling out, and that part almost said: 'go ahead.'

But then a rush of other thoughts flooded my mind. Not that any of them were comparable to my situation, but examples of other athletes who chose to go on when they had every excuse to stop – from pros to the just-under-17 hour finishers. Somehow they continued, walking it in, and I had always respected that.

'If I touch you, you're out,' the paramedic reiterated. 'Not yet, then', I replied, rolling over onto my knees and elbows. At that moment I caught a glimpse of runners continuing past, and for the first time, realized that my chances for Kona in this race had exploded minutes earlier. 'You think about it,' the paramedic urged, and I moved to a sitting position, where I did just that. The pieces of the last few minutes finally came together: from Kona to disaster in just a few minutes, completely beyond my control. What now?

I gave up. 'I'm done,' I said. It wasn't worth it. What did I have to prove? I'd finished plenty of these races before. I would have other chances. Why continue when it feels this risky? No regrets, I decided. But . . .

'No, wait!' I halted, 'can't give up just yet.' The ambulance radio crackled – another emergency. 'Jump in, or we've got to go,' said the paramedic. 'Go', I said instinctively. 'I'll just walk a little.'

Off they went, and there I was, having lost several minutes on the side of the road, as in my worst nightmare. Woozy, deflated, 11 miles to go to the finish line, certainly toward a personal worst. At that moment, the thought of actually covering those 11 miles seemed impossible, insane. So I took one step at a time, and remained upright. Crushed and unsure of myself, I tried to find reasons to keep going.

As my mind cleared, I began thinking about the reasons I started Ironman racing – to finish. I remembered advice I had given friends who were on the course in the process of completing their first Ironman: your race plan may shift, but you will finish. I knew they probably would spend hours walking today. I thought about the people who would be walking long after dark, refusing to give in to temptation to stop. Maybe I could do that, too.

So I decided that this would be an entirely different Ironman finish. At least different than the ones I had completed in recent years. I would walk the entire 11 miles, I decided, and be part of the broader community of athletes who are not there for personal bests or Kona slots, but for the pride and joy of finishing. I would follow their lead, it was the best I could do.

Occasionally I tried to jog on miles 17 and 18, but I immediately felt it in my chest. 'Too much, too risky, just walk', I told myself. And I did. I reached the turnaround at State Street, slowly walking to the spot that in 2002 and 2003 had seen me running and picking up energy. Between the time on the ground and the time walking, it had taken me 80 minutes to cover the 6 miles from the halfway point to State Street.

But then a small something clicked. At the turn, the mile marker said: 19. This development stunned me – 'hey, I'm almost done, I've covered 19 miles! Maybe it's time to try to jog again.' And I did, slowly, trying to find peace in my body with a pace that did not push my lungs. Step by faster step, it was working, and I kept going onto the lakefront path. By the time I reached the second turnaround at mile 22, I was actually running. I looked at my watch, did some math, and realized if I ran at a reasonable pace, I might actually finish under 11 hours.

Then I thought back to the years where sub-11 seems light years away. In those days, I couldn't imagine how athletes accomplished that kind of speed as I happily struggled through those 11 and 12 hour finishes. The day I broke 11 hours, at Ironman Florida 2001, I felt like a different person. I decided, nothing risky, but I would try to break eleven hours on this day.

I started running back to Madison, toward the finish line. An hour earlier, I was on my way into an ambulance, ready to give up. Suddenly, I was going to finish. How did all this happen?

I felt a different kind of pride as I ran the last four miles to the finish. It was a pride that undoubtedly hundreds of first timers and other Ironman finishers felt as they approached the same finish line before me and long after me. It's a long hard day for everyone out there, and everyone finds it in themselves to make it through challenges and adversity in their own way. Sometimes the right decision is to step aside, save it for another day. Nearly 200 racers made that choice, and for them it was the right one. Nearly 2000 others found the meaning of Ironman that day as they made it to the finish line chute, smiled broadly, and crossed the line.

Finish

The finish line of an Ironman race is a special place. I have always crossed it with arms held high and strong, proud of the way I had covered the course, whether it was in 10, 11, 12, 13 or almost 14 hours. But when I was shuffling along miles earlier, thinking I would have to walk the rest of the way, I told myself I would cross the line, but not hold my arms high. In those walking miles, I did not feel worthy of that kind of display. But in the final hour, as I pulled it together from the lowest low to nearly the highest high of the day, I changed my mind: this was a race and a finish like no other. I absolutely deserved to finish with pride, arms held high.

I crossed the line of my 22nd Ironman triathlon in 10:52:30, 122nd overall, 14th M40-44 (13 minutes from a Kona slot). I felt the crush of disappointment in not reaching my Kona qualifying goal, but exceptional pride about having finished at all.

For all I experienced out there on the course on this day, it could have been my first time. But as I tell friends who ask: the point isn't the number of Ironman finishes. The point is that no matter how many Ironman races any of us have done, you're likely to experience something completely unexpected in any Ironman race, something that will further define your character. It's why we race, and that's exactly what happened at Ironman Wisconsin 2004.

Ironman Wisconsin 2005:
What Drives You?

What Drives You?

It's a simple question. A question I asked myself during the run portion of the 2005 Ironman Wisconsin. It was also the opposite of another question I was asking myself at the same time: why do you need to suffer like this? I searched for an answer, and realized that my answer to the questions has varied widely over the years.

Then I wondered about all the triathletes on the race course around me. How would they a nswer the questions: What drives you? What gets you in the pool, on the bike, or on the run, day after day? What are you hoping for? And do you get what you want?

Some of you were there in Wisconsin. The rest of you – admit it – have your own good responses for those questions based on your training and racing experience. I want to know how all of you would answer.

The Ironman Wisconsin 2005 was a tough race for me, one of those races where you need to dig deep to find reasons to keep going. The swim was fine, and I had one of the better bike splits on the day. It could only get better, right?

Well, not necessarily. It fell apart for me on the run. The bike course was very windy and very hot. I had tried to stay hydrated, felt ok, and my self-assessment in the final miles of the bike said that I had a good run in me. Passing the two mile point of this two loop run course, I still thought it was going well.

Then out of the blue, things felt out of sync. I felt a desperate need to just stop and walk to get more oxygen in my body. The kind of walk where you are just breathing as deep as you can, trying to fill the lungs as much air as possible. But relief wasn't going to come anytime soon. And I've raced enough times to decide that things were getting risky, I wasn't going to push myself into trouble. Life is too short.

So, in a déjà vu of last year on the same course, I found myself alternating between walking and running, with plenty of time to think. That's when I began wondering: why do I continue to make myself suffer like this? What more is there to prove?

I know I am not alone. At one point or another, all of us have asked ourselves the same questions. And most of us have great answers that keep us going. In the heat of the day --a day in which nearly 400 racers did not finish – I sensed that many of the people I was racing with were having the same internal conversation sometime.

But things can change, the nearer one gets to the end of the race. Get to that finish line, those internal conversations can cease, and for many, dreams are made reality.

A few hours after finishing my own 2005 Ironman Wisconsin, I went back to the finish line to see some of those dreams come true. There is no better place to witness the range of human emotion than at the finish of an Ironman triathlon. Smiles, tears, hugs, laughter, pain, agony, elation, disappointment; it's all there.

It's one thing to watch people running the final steps towards the hallowed finish line, seeing them get a jolt of adrenaline, high-fiving the crowd until they cross the line to cheers and the flash of cameras documenting the accomplishment of a lifetime.

But it's another thing altogether to witness things from the other side of the finish line, after they cross the line. What happens after the flashbulbs go off?

I positioned myself just behind the finish line photographers and among the volunteer 'catchers', who, two-by-two, readied themselves to greet and sometimes hold up each new finisher. I spent more than an hour there, taking in the finishers who came in just under 14 hours, and those who were able to beat the 15 hour marker. In between, I saw some awesome things.

After the racers crossed the line, cameras flashed, catchers caught, and medal people placed the medal around the neck of finishers, my overall observation was: these people are amazingly happy. Not just smiling for the finish line camera and then dropping their guard. But truly happy.

For some people, finishing seemed like the greatest gift they had given themselves in their lives. What lucky people.

Some of the things I saw:

- The man whose wife jumped into his arms, hugging him with such excitement that it seemed he might break; he, in turn, was smiling as happily as anyone I have ever seen
- The finishers who, after pumping their fists for the camera, kept clenching them in excitement, silently saying to themselves through a clenched smile: YES!
- The woman who broke into sobs of happiness and could not stop
- The mother, grinning ear-to-ear, running with her son who was wearing a shirt that said: Go Susan; she had done just that
- The father who led his family across the line, laughing as the kids crossed before him; a scene repeated over, clear pictures of family unity and support around the goal
- The runners who charged through the finish line so fast that they could not stop, as if they were trying to smash through a previously unsurpassable barrier; the volunteers literally had to block and catch them, with a smile on their face each time

These racers and finishers had been on the course for 14 or 15 hours. They undoubtedly had tough moments on the race course. But they made it to the end with such enthusiasm and such life that few, if anyone, observing could not help but be inspired. I, too, was inspired by them.

They clearly were driven. Driven to sign up for the event 364 days earlier. Driven to train all year. Driven to start the race. Some were driven to the edge during the day. Others were driven to finish, no matter what. All of them were driven, in their own way.

Ironman Wisconsin 2006:
Observations From the Sidelines

I had never watched an Ironman race. I've always been a participant, more than two dozen times. Until Ironman Wisconsin 2006.

For the last five years, at 7am on the second Sunday of September, I've been at the starting line of Ironman Wisconsin, in Madison. This year was no exception, except this time I stood on dry land, rather than treading water in Lake Monona, site of the Ironman swim. After eleven years of near-constant training and racing, I had decided to take a break from serious competition.

I looked forward to becoming a spectator and a race photographer in Madison, watching athletes work hard while I stood comfortably on the side of the course, happy that it wasn't me out there. However, my attitude shifted throughout the cold, rainy and windy day.

Here's what it felt like to be watching an Ironman for the first time.

Swim

The race began with an Ironman record 2475 participants starting the swim at 7am. My son Eric and I positioned ourselves on shore, to the right side of the starting line.

It's a truly beautiful but also bewildering sight to see that many athletes begin to swim at once. It's a solid wave of white, grey and black; of arms, legs and heads turning to breathe. You wonder how they survive the first few minutes. Everybody's in everybody's way. It's a mess. It's quite a sight.

And I knew, for many in the water, it was quite scary. It took me years to get over feeling of panic in the water during those first battling minutes. The water churns all around you like a washing machine, you get hit all over (unintentionally of course), you try to maintain smooth breathing. And it's hard. I was glad I was watching, not swimming.

Not more than two minutes after the race had started, something strange happened. It seemed that a swimmer had veered completely off course, and was going to swim right into the grassy shore. But it was no accident.

This male swimmer, maybe in his 40s and a little on the heavy side, beached himself, and was helped out of the water by spectators. He was completely disoriented, and pointed to his chest. He felt like he was having a heart attack. After sitting on a bench, though, it was clear he had panicked.

I'm not sure he ever returned to the water. A year's worth of training, done in 100 meters. Thirty eight other swimmers, possibly a record, would not complete the swim by the cutoff time, either.

But the rest of the swimmers made it all the way, with swim times of 50 minutes all the way to the swim cutoff of more than two hours.

Swim to Bike Transition

I am always disoriented when I exit the water, my head spinning as I try to navigate my way through transition and onto the bike. So it was with interest that Eric and I were positioned for a good view of athletes as they came out of the water.

The air temperature was a chilly 55 degrees. Spectators huddled in

jackets and hats, as swimmers ran by in Speedos, wetsuits flung over their shoulders.

I was surprised to see how alert and fast athletes of all ages, sizes and abilities seemed as they entered transition. Out of the water, they immediately ran to wetsuit removers, then ran up a four-level parking garage helix to the indoor transition area.

Everyone seemed to be running so fast. I've always felt I was moving in slow motion. Maybe I've appeared more together than I felt? The earlier finishers were simply sprinting toward their bikes. People shooting for Kona slots, possibly. They had a look of great intensity, one that said: every second counts. I knew that feeling, too.

Next, determined triathletes emerged from the changing rooms, many wearing cold-weather cycling apparel. I've often been one of the few to seemingly overdress on the bike course, wearing a vest and arm warmers on cold race days, while most everyone else remains in a tank top. I was pleased to see many in jackets and heavy gloves. They would need it out on the course.

Bike

The Ironman Wisconsin bike course has always been deceptively challenging. It lacks the long, steeps climbs of Ironman Canada or Lake Placid. On an elevation chart, it looks very tame, just a little harder than Ironman Florida. But it is made up of relentless hills that never let up. The course breaks you apart slowly, hill by hill.

Eric and I drove immediately to my favorite part of the bike course, what I call the Roller Coaster hills on Garfoot Road, at about the 37 mile point. It's a series of three short but steep declines and inclines, where you scream down the hill, then fight your way up the other side over and over and over. Eric and I positioned ourselves at the top of the last climb.

The riders looked fairly miserable, as they navigated the climb. The rain was picking up, winds were blowing harder, and the temperature was locked solidly in the middle 50s. It was not pleasant, and they had 75 miles to go.

But the perseverance on the face of every rider that passed us was inspiring. Knowing how it felt to be at that point, in those conditions, it was clear that their mental strength would be every bit as important as their physical strength on this difficult day.

Then Eric and I jumped in the comfortably warm car, with windshield wipers batting away rain, and drove east to the 45 mile point, a flat part of the course on at Mineral Point Road that comes just after the nastiest of the course's climbs.

Once we got there, the conditions were no better, and it was clear they were taking a toll on the riders who were deeper into the bike course. It was the kind of day where you wouldn't blame people for packing it up and quitting early. But on they rode, past Eric, me and other appreciative spectators brandishing umbrellas at the side of the road. I continued to be glad I was watching, and not on the course. It looked hard, and it was.

After a break, Eric and I returned to the same spot two hours later to see pros now at the 85 mile point of the race. Chris McDonald blasted through the intersection ten minutes ahead of his next competitor, Markus Foster. But it wasn't just the pros passing us.

There was a constant stream of people who were still on their first lap, at least three hours and 40 miles behind the pros. These were the true back-of-the-packers, the athletes who would be on the course for 14, 15, 16 or 17 hours. They kept their eyes forward, pedaling slowly but steadily, without complaint. It was easy to admire the fast pros, but more important to recognize the sheer toughness of these slower riders for continuing.

Bike to Run Transition

We left the athletes on the soggy roads west of Madison, and returned to the transition area to welcome the first pros and age groupers. Even though we had a car, lead pro Chris McDonald beat us back to the transition area on his bike, and was just stepping onto the run course as we arrived. He headed up the cruel incline at the start of the marathon course looking as if he hadn't ridden at all. Too smooth, too easy. Remarkable.

Eric and I made our way to the bike drop off point to watch other riders return: Markus Forster, Katja Schumacher, Hilary Biscay, Andrea Fisher. Then the age groupers started arriving.

My first steps off the bike are always difficult. I feel as if I can barely walk, and it seems like I'm barely hobbling to the changing area. So I was constantly surprised to see athlete after athlete hop off their bike and run into the transition area with little difficulty. One athlete cramped up – that seemed like me. Otherwise, they all looked like they felt great, rushing along to the next part of the race.

Run

I don't know how the time flew by so fast, but by the time Eric and I made it to the run course, Chris McDonald had completed nearly 13 miles, and was approaching us looking as comfortable as he had when he started the run. But about two minutes behind him, Markus Forster was closing in fast, having cut McDonald's lead by 8 minutes. About half an hour later, Katja Schumacher charged past us, solidly in the lead of the women's race.

Eric and I turned our attention to the age group runners beginning their marathon, heading west down State Street. I could not believe how fast they seemed to be running. Runner after runner, male or female, they seemed smooth and steady.

Now, I've done way too many Ironman races and I know it does not feel good on that first mile of the marathon, or on many of them, for that matter. But I also know that I tend to run pretty fast first miles, too. And I know how hard it is to concentrate on one step after the other, fighting the discomfort the whole way. These runners were doing it, almost smiling. It kept raining, they kept running and smiling.

And for the first time all day, I began to get envious. I found myself wishing I could be out there, running too. What was most impressive was that each and every racer in the marathon had braved challenging swim and bike conditions, fought through them to get to this point, a point that got them closer to an Ironman Finisher's medal with each step.

And that's what it's all about. It's all about the finish. It's why we do what we do; it's why we train, why we suffer, why we race, why we smile, why we thrive.

Reflection

It was a tough day that led to very slow times, including the slowest winning time in Ironman Wisconsin history. But at the end of the day, it wasn't about speed or finish times. It was about how the athletes made it 141.6 miles on a cold, rainy, windy Madison day, and became an Ironman, each and every one of them.

And I realized that being an Ironman at the end of the day was far, far better than having had a comfortable time watching it. Observing was a fascinating experience, and I'll do it again. But I'll also look forward to the time my competitive break is over, and I return to the Ironman course.

The next day I signed up for Ironman Wisconsin 2007.

Ironman Wisconsin 2007:
Rider's-Eye Perspective

On September 9, 2007, I returned to complete my fifth Ironman Wisconsin, my 29th Ironman race since July 1997. This time, I wanted to do something different. Experience the Ironman in a unique way. And I did: I shot photos on the bike course, and I tracked the entire 112-mile ride with a Garmin 405 GPS Watch. As a result, the 2007 experience presented here gets to the nuts and bolts of the bike course, perhaps Ironman Wisconsin's most daunting feature.

To many triathletes, the Ironman Wisconsin bike course has appeared relatively easier than other north American courses such as Ironman USA Lake Placid and Ironman Canada. But when triathletes arrive to race Ironman Wisconsin, they are inevitably surprised at the difficulty they face on the bike course.

While the elevation changes on paper are quite more significant in Lake Placid, the tricky subtleties in Wisconsin make it such that an overall bike split on both courses can be very similar.

What the Ironman Wisconsin bike course lacks in vertical elevation challenges, it more than compensates with the challenge of never letting up; the course chips away at you with a continuous series of slight gains, turns, and technical challenges that constantly serve to damper hopes for a bike course PR.

Personal Race Data Summary

My overall bike split in Ironman Wisconsin 2007 was 5 hours, 53 minutes and 57 seconds. First 56 miles: 2:52:49 riding time, 19.44 mph; second 56 miles: 3:01:08 riding time, 18.68 mph. Equipment: Softride Rocket 650TT, Zipp 909 wheels, Sidi shoes, Look pedals, 2 bottle cages and 2 pouches. Fueling: 4 PowerBars and 8 GU packets on bike; bananas every other aid station; water/Gatorade every aid station. Hammer Factor: limited; I rode comfortably; never pushed it too hard, never bonked, never suffered.

Ironman Wisconsin 112-Mile Bike Course: Rider's Perspective

The 112 mile Ironman Wisconsin bike course starts fun and fast, then gradually eats away at you over the miles. It throws no serious difficulty your way, but it refuses to yield over most of the course. Go out too fast, and you can suffer later.

With that as a sort of warning, the first 16 or so miles, out to the two-loop section, are a good warm-up, taking riders to the west of Madison, from the small city toward classic Midwestern farmland. Some small rollers stretch your leg muscles, and a couple of pretty steep but short downhills will give you a speed boost, but also provide warning that they may hurt you a little on the way back. Here's my data from those first miles:

Reaching the 39-mile loop section, you'll continue west on relatively tame terrain until you approach the town of Mt. Horeb. Approaching mile 30, you'll be faced with about a 1⁄2 mile long climb that veers to the left then right, where you'll be greeted by aid station volunteers. Get what you need, then prepare for five miles of work.

Miles 30 to 35 (and 70 to 75 on the return trip) take riders through relentless up-down riding that I like to call The Rollercoasters of Witte Road and Garfoot Road. Passing between and through farms, these miles toss it all at you: fast declines followed immediately by sharp uphills again and again, with short stretches of reasonably flat road connecting the little challenges.

Complete 112 Mile Ride

Segment	Segment Stats			Cumulative Stats		
	Miles	Ride Time	MPH	Miles	Ride Time	MPH
112.4 Miles	112.4	5:53:57	19.05	112.4	5:53:57	19.05

56-mile Segments

Segment	Segment Stats			Cumulative Stats		
	Miles	Ride Time	MPH	Miles	Ride Time	MPH
1 to 56	56.0	2:52:49	19.44	56.0	2:52:49	19.44
57 to 112.4	56.4	3:01:08	18.68	112.4	5:53:57	19.05

Comparable Course Segments

Segment	Segment Stats			Cumulative Stats		
	Miles	Ride Time	MPH	Miles	Ride Time	MPH
Outbound	16.0	0:49:09	19.53	16.0	0:49:09	19.53
Lap 1	40.0	2:03:40	19.41	56.0	2:52:49	19.44
Lap 2	40.0	2:08:28	18.68	96.0	5:01:17	19.12
Inbound	16.4	0:52:40	18.66	112.4	5:53:57	19.05

Mile	Split	Mile MPH	MaxMPH	Ascent	Descent	Ride Time	Ride MPH
1	3:47	15.9	26.4	50	90	0:03:47	15.9
2	3:36	16.7	22.5	52	62	0:07:23	16.3
3	2:55	20.6	24.0	52	53	0:10:18	17.5
4	2:36	23.1	30.0	25	52	0:12:54	18.6
5	2:57	20.3	23.8	45	3	0:15:51	18.9
6	2:52	20.9	24.0	54	28	0:18:43	19.2
7	2:31	23.8	29.2	35	25	0:21:14	19.8
8	3:03	19.7	28.0	87	4	0:24:17	19.8
9	3:07	19.3	25.1	78	24	0:27:24	19.7
10	3:38	16.5	25.2	118	29	0:31:02	19.3
11	2:14	26.9	34.0	23	115	0:33:16	19.8
12	3:17	18.3	24.3	62	6	0:36:33	19.7
13	2:59	20.1	25.3	20	28	0:39:32	19.7
14	2:18	26.1	32.5	11	49	0:41:50	20.1
15	2:44	22.0	25.4	15	56	0:44:34	20.2
16	4:35	13.1	25.9	23	30	0:49:09	19.5

At first, it's fun. Then getting over the next hill gets tougher each time. You'll think you're done, then there's more. You'll see when you get there. You don't want to be bonking the second time you ride this section. It's a bad place to be on the rocks.

Next up is a slightly dangerous fast, swerving downhill on northern Garfoot Road. You'll wish you can take it at full-speed, but only the most expert of riders can do it. It's too easy to lose control on the sharp turns here. Sacrifice a few seconds for better control.

The course flattens out on the top half, east-bound road for a few miles, allowing you to relax a little. You'll need the break, because when you make a right turn at Country Road KP to begin a southward path toward the start of loop two, the course's most challenging climbs await.

The climbs – at Old Sauk Pass and on Timber Lane – aren't very long, but they can be quite taxing. When you arrive there, settle into your easiest gear, sit back, and pedal as efficiently as you can.

Stay steady for the next few miles until you reach the town of Verona, where you'll be greeted by a cheering crowd that treats you as if you are a Tour de France rider. Savor the moments, smile at spectators and enjoy your short time there. Because after it's over, you get to do it all again on lap 2.

You'll finish lap 2 at about 95 miles, with 17 more to go. Depending on the heat, wind and your nutrition and hydration at that point, those last miles may be relatively breezy or can be very challenging.

Don't let the apparent downhill back to town on the race website course map fool you. It's more work that you'll expect. Be prepared mentally and physically at that point, and you'll do fine.

Mile	Split	Mile MPH	MaxMPH	Ascent	Descent	Ride Time	Ride MPH
17	5:36	10.7	32.3	68	94	0:54:45	18.6
18	3:03	19.7	37.2	111	98	0:57:48	18.7
19	2:58	20.2	29.6	46	47	1:00:46	18.8
20	2:37	22.9	25.1	17	2	1:03:23	18.9
21	3:01	19.9	25.8	55	10	1:06:24	19.0
22	3:25	17.6	26.2	100	24	1:09:49	18.9
23	2:14	26.9	33.0	25	147	1:12:03	19.2
24	2:48	21.4	29.2	42	41	1:14:51	19.2
25	3:11	18.8	23.9	57	41	1:18:02	19.2
26	2:53	20.8	31.6	95	78	1:20:55	19.3
27	3:14	18.6	24.9	118	37	1:24:09	19.3
28	3:10	18.9	21.2	63	46	1:27:19	19.2
29	4:25	13.6	20.5	148	9	1:31:44	19.0
30	3:10	18.9	25.4	51	59	1:34:54	19.0
31	2:51	21.1	26.1	35	41	1:37:45	19.0
32	2:29	24.2	37.9	103	185	1:40:14	19.2
33	3:26	17.5	37.2	120	68	1:43:40	19.1
34	3:50	15.7	32.9	122	79	1:47:30	19.0
35	3:24	17.6	28.9	89	132	1:50:54	18.9
36	2:01	29.8	36.3	26	189	1:52:55	19.1
37	2:35	23.2	30.1	42	43	1:55:30	19.2
38	2:50	21.2	26.7	38	26	1:58:20	19.3
39	2:49	21.3	27.3	28	55	2:01:09	19.3
40	2:56	20.5	23.1	35	24	2:04:05	19.3
41	2:57	20.3	23.0	66	29	2:07:02	19.4
42	2:49	21.3	27.3	18	48	2:09:51	19.4
43	2:56	20.5	24.0	23	14	2:12:47	19.4
44	4:01	14.9	21.9	152	48	2:16:48	19.3
45	4:51	12.4	25.0	152	91	2:21:39	19.1
46	3:15	18.5	34.1	91	78	2:24:54	19.0
47	2:33	23.5	28.6	40	23	2:27:27	19.1
48	1:59	30.3	44.1	28	166	2:29:26	19.3
49	3:45	16.0	33.6	153	35	2:33:11	19.2
50	3:05	19.5	40.5	71	170	2:36:16	19.2
51	2:32	23.7	40.6	78	46	2:38:48	19.3
52	2:32	23.7	31.1	28	21	2:41:20	19.3
53	2:45	21.8	27.9	26	21	2:44:05	19.4
54	2:54	20.7	26.2	3	79	2:46:59	19.4
55	3:07	19.3	21.9	13	8	2:50:06	19.4
56	2:43	22.1	25.7	55	22	2:52:49	19.4

Mile	Split	Mile MPH	MaxMPH	Ascent	Descent	Ride Time	Ride MPH
57	2:49	21.3	23.7	29	60	2:55:38	19.5
58	2:40	22.5	27.6	18	34	2:58:18	19.5
59	3:20	18.0	26.0	98	20	3:01:38	19.5
60	3:24	17.6	35.1	100	62	3:05:02	19.5
61	2:53	20.8	36.9	69	68	3:07:55	19.5
62	2:42	22.2	27.8	25	8	3:10:37	19.5
63	2:59	20.1	23.1	30	6	3:13:36	19.5
64	3:25	17.6	25.6	124	63	3:17:01	19.5
65	2:56	20.5	32.2	70	104	3:19:57	19.5
66	2:27	24.5	31.9	25	90	3:22:24	19.6
67	2:52	20.9	26.0	31	8	3:25:16	19.6
68	3:24	17.6	28.2	69	54	3:28:40	19.6
69	3:24	17.6	26.3	88	67	3:32:04	19.5
70	3:23	17.7	22.0	67	13	3:35:27	19.5
71	4:47	12.5	18.5	162	11	3:40:14	19.3
72	3:44	16.1	24.7	54	48	3:43:58	19.3
73	3:04	19.6	23.1	33	9	3:47:02	19.3
74	3:01	19.9	31.7	61	106	3:50:03	19.3
75	3:14	18.6	35.4	91	127	3:53:17	19.3
76	3:59	15.1	30.9	128	105	3:57:16	19.2
77	4:14	14.2	24.7	119	90	4:01:30	19.1
78	2:21	25.5	35.5	11	269	4:03:51	19.2
79	2:38	22.8	29.7	33	91	4:06:29	19.2
80	2:55	20.6	23.9	10	40	4:09:24	19.2
81	3:14	18.6	24.4	41	50	4:12:38	19.2
82	3:04	19.6	22.6	34	9	4:15:42	19.2
83	3:17	18.3	21.8	54	9	4:18:59	19.2
84	2:56	20.5	25.4	18	44	4:21:55	19.2
85	3:04	19.6	23.8	25	14	4:24:59	19.2
86	3:11	18.8	23.4	26	21	4:28:10	19.2
87	6:03	9.9	24.3	200	53	4:34:13	19.0
88	3:45	16.0	33.5	123	65	4:37:58	19.0
89	2:30	24.0	30.0	21	17	4:40:28	19.0
90	2:37	22.9	32.3	57	112	4:43:05	19.1
91	2:24	25.0	41.2	40	81	4:45:29	19.1
92	5:15	11.4	22.4	190	6	4:50:44	19.0
93	2:15	26.7	39.8	53	133	4:52:59	19.0
94	2:43	22.1	29.8	44	32	4:55:42	19.1
95	2:41	22.4	27.8	38	67	4:58:23	19.1
96	2:54	20.7	26.1	23	66	5:01:17	19.1

Mile	Split	Mile MPH	MaxMPH	Ascent	Descent	Ride Time	Ride MPH
97	3:05	19.5	21.9	7	30	5:04:22	19.1
98	2:47	21.6	23.9	3	17	5:07:09	19.1
99	3:49	15.7	21.0	131	20	5:10:58	19.1
100	3:30	17.1	26.6	62	59	5:14:28	19.1
101	2:54	20.7	29.7	14	75	5:17:22	19.1
102	3:07	19.3	26.9	45	16	5:20:29	19.1
103	3:56	15.3	32.5	106	108	5:24:25	19.0
104	2:39	22.6	28.7	27	64	5:27:04	19.1
105	2:32	23.7	29.9	17	104	5:29:36	19.1
106	3:10	18.9	28.5	74	65	5:32:46	19.1
107	3:23	17.7	20.5	18	50	5:36:09	19.1
108	2:53	20.8	26.3	18	50	5:39:02	19.1
109	3:07	19.3	21.6	52	33	5:42:09	19.1
110	3:35	16.7	23.9	48	68	5:45:44	19.1
111	3:30	17.1	21.2	25	44	5:49:14	19.1
112	2:58	20.2	21.5	38	14	5:52:12	19.1
Helix	1:45	13.0	16.0	47	32	5:53:57	19.1

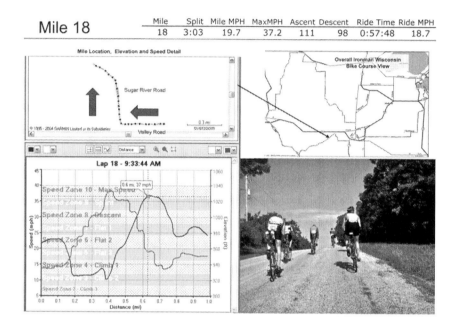

Bike Course Technical Overview and Details

With data and bike course overview from my 2007 race as background, the following charts delve into the details of selected key spots on the course: helix start, outbound ride, rolling hills at Witte Road, Old Sauk Pass, Verona, the return to Old Sauk Pass at mile 86, etc. It's a good sample of what you should expect on the bike course.

Each chart contains comprehensive information about the characteristics and performance of that mile using real-time GPS data and in-race photos.

The bar of data across the top of each mile page contains an overview of the mile and my data: elevation change, my average speed and maximum speed during that mile, mile split, time elapsed overall, cumulative average speed to that point.

The left side of the page has two charts detailing the location and direction of the mile on the course route (top), and the second-by-second measurement of elevation changes and my speed (bottom). This elevation/speed chart is the key: it tells you what to expect in terms of course terrain and how you should plan to ride it.

The right side of the page contains the overall bike course map, linked to the specific mile, so you know where on the course the action takes place (top). The bottom right section is the rider's eye view of a key part in the mile. Taken with my bike-mounted camera, these photos show you what to expect when you get there. Combined with all the other data, you've got the tools you need to map your bike course strategy.

These pages are excerpts from the new book Epic Ride;: The Legendary Ironman Bike Course Guide, which details all 112 miles of the Ironman Wisconsin bike course, and more.

Epic Ride: Ironman Bike Course Strategies

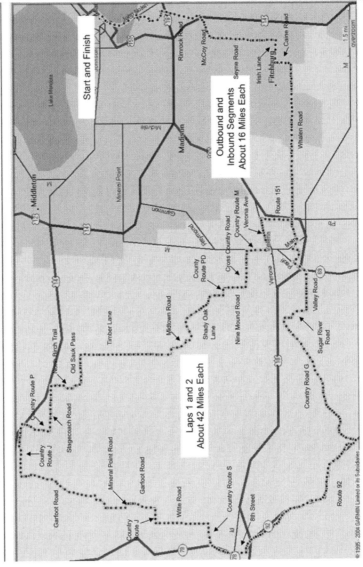

Ironman Wisconsin Bike Course Map

Start and Finish

Outbound and Inbound Segments About 16 Miles Each

Laps 1 and 2 About 42 Miles Each

Measured Live with Garmin GPS By Raymond Britt #1000 during Ironman Wisconsin 2007

Personal Race Data Summary

- Overall Bike Split: 5 hours, 53 minutes and 57 seconds; summary data below
- Equipment: Softride Rocket 650TT, Zipp 909 wheels, Sidi shoes, Look pedals, 2 bottle cages and 2 pouches
- Fueling: 4 PowerBars and 8 GU packets on bike; bananas every other aid station; water/Gatorade every aid station
- Hammer Factor: I did not hammer, I rode comfortably; never pushed it too hard, never bonked, never suffered

Complete 112 Mile Ride

Segment	Segment Stats			Cumulative Stats		
	Miles	Ride Time	MPH	Miles	Ride Time	MPH
112.4 Miles	112.4	5:53:57	19.05	112.4	5:53:57	19.05

56-mile Segments

Segment	Segment Stats			Cumulative Stats		
	Miles	Ride Time	MPH	Miles	Ride Time	MPH
1 to 56	56.0	2:52:49	19.44	56.0	2:52:49	19.44
57 to 112.4	56.4	3:01:08	18.68	112.4	5:53:57	19.05

Comparable Course Segments

Segment	Segment Stats			Cumulative Stats		
	Miles	Ride Time	MPH	Miles	Ride Time	MPH
Outbound	16.0	0:49:09	19.53	16.0	0:49:09	19.53
Lap 1	40.0	2:03:40	19.41	56.0	2:52:49	19.44
Lap 2	40.0	2:08:28	18.68	96.0	5:01:17	19.12
Inbound	16.4	0:52:40	18.66	112.4	5:53:57	19.05

It All Starts Here: Transition

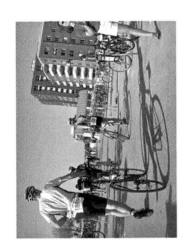

Mile by Mile Page Content Guide

On the next 112 pages, each mile is analyzed on a detailed page, based on my 2007 race performance as measured on a Garmin 305 GPS watch, photos, course experience, and additional technical analysis.

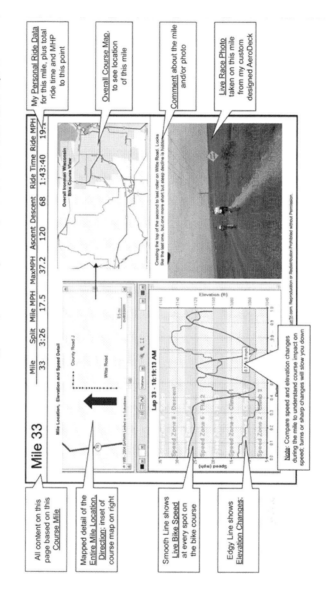

All content on this page based on this **Course Mile**

Mapped detail of the **Entire Mile Location, Direction**; inset of course map on right

Smooth Line shows **Live Bike Speed** at every spot on the bike course

Edgy Line shows **Elevation Changes**

My Personal Ride Data for this mile, plus total ride time and MHP to this point

Overall Course Map to see location of this mile

Comment about the mile and/or photo

Live Race Photo taken on this mile from my custom designed AeroDeck

Note: Compare speed and elevation changes during the mile to understand course impact on speed; turns or sharp changes will slow you down

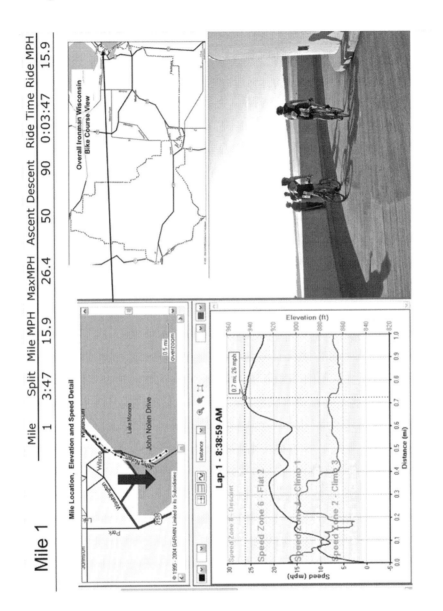

Mile	Split	Mile MPH	MaxMPH	Ascent	Descent	Ride Time	Ride MPH
1	3:47	15.9	26.4	50	90	0:03:47	15.9

Mile 1

Mile	Split	Mile MPH	MaxMPH	Ascent	Descent	Ride Time	Ride MPH
5	2:57	20.3	23.8	45	3	0:15:51	18.9

Mile 5

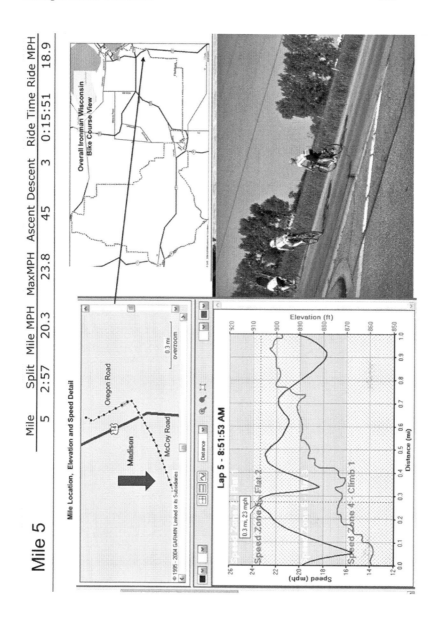

Mile	Split	Mile MPH	MaxMPH	Ascent	Descent	Ride Time	Ride MPH
9	3:07	19.3	25.1	78	24	0:27:24	19.7

Mile 9

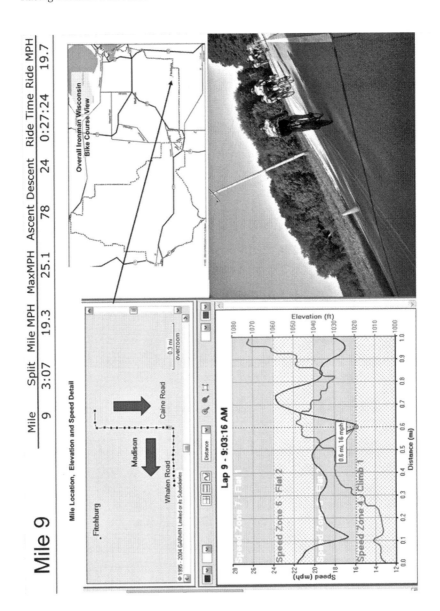

Mile 10

Mile	Split	Mile MPH	MaxMPH	Ascent	Descent	Ride Time	Ride MPH
10	3:38	16.5	25.2	118	29	0:31:02	19.3

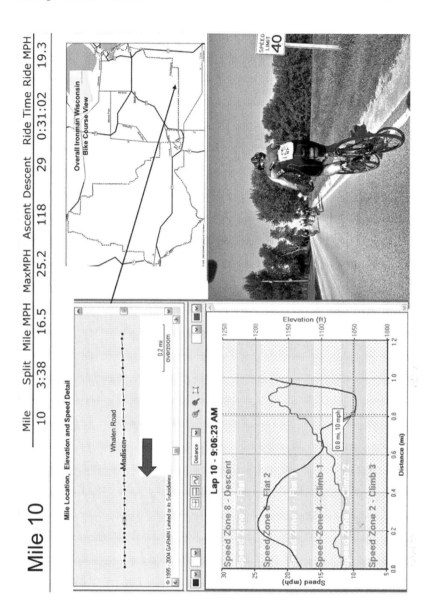

Mile 10 Detail: Taking the First Whalen Road Hill

Mile 10 Detail: Taking the First Whalen Road Hill

Mile 10 Detail: Taking the First Whalen Road Hill

Mile 11

Mile	Split	Mile MPH	MaxMPH	Ascent	Descent	Ride Time	Ride MPH
11	2:14	26.9	34.0	23	115	0:33:16	19.8

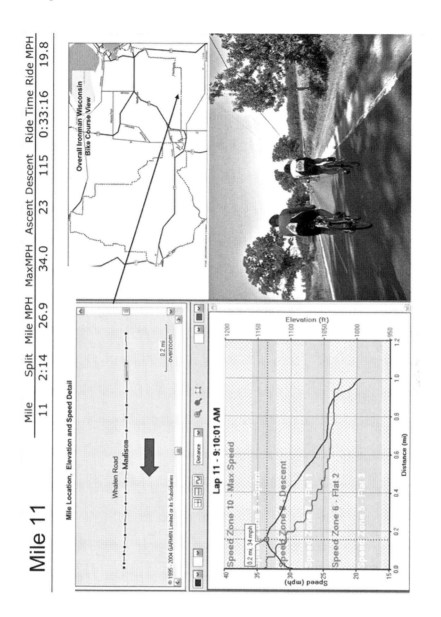

Mile 18

Mile	Split	Mile MPH	MaxMPH	Ascent	Descent	Ride Time	Ride MPH
18	3:03	19.7	37.2	111	98	0:57:48	18.7

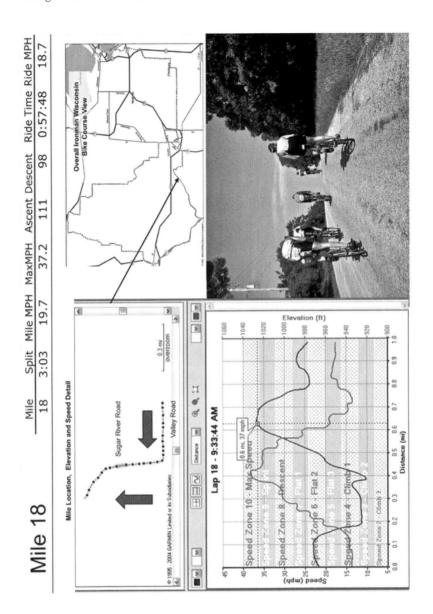

Mile 22

Mile	Split	Mile MPH	MaxMPH	Ascent	Descent	Ride Time	Ride MPH
22	3:25	17.6	26.2	100	24	1:09:49	18.9

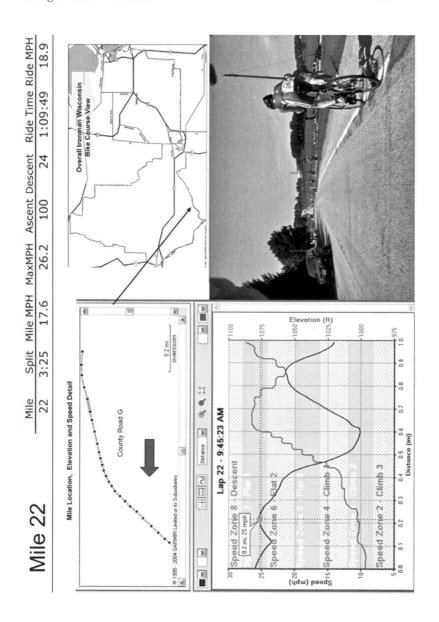

Mile 24

Mile	Split	Mile MPH	MaxMPH	Ascent	Descent	Ride Time	Ride MPH
24	2:48	21.4	29.2	42	41	1:14:51	19.2

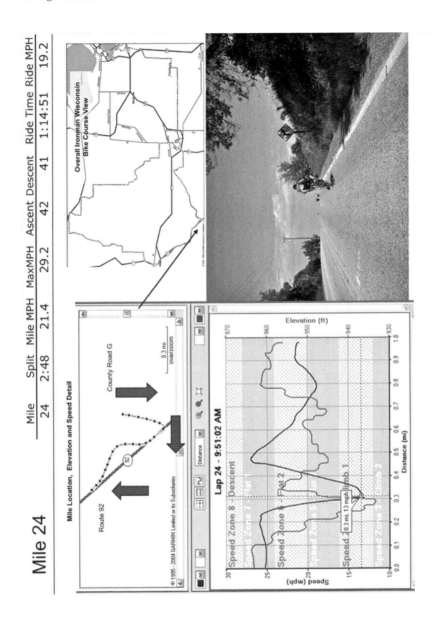

Mile	Split	Mile MPH	MaxMPH	Ascent	Descent	Ride Time	Ride MPH
29	4:25	13.6	20.5	148	9	1:31:44	19.0

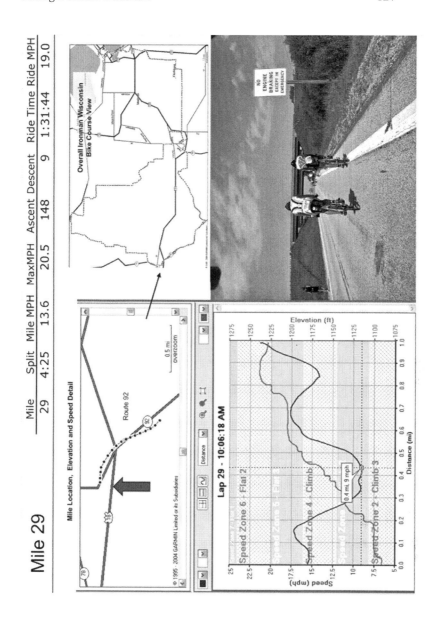

Mile 29

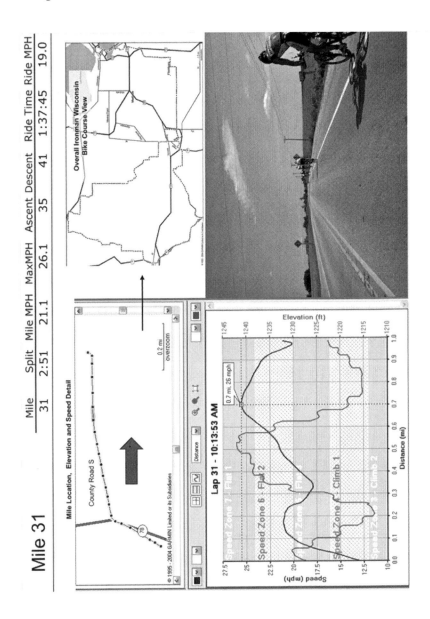

Mile	Split	Mile MPH	MaxMPH	Ascent	Descent	Ride Time	Ride MPH
31	2:51	21.1	26.1	35	41	1:37:45	19.0

Mile 31

Mile	Split	Mile MPH	MaxMPH	Ascent	Descent	Ride Time	Ride MPH
32	2:29	24.2	37.9	103	185	1:40:14	19.2

Mile 32

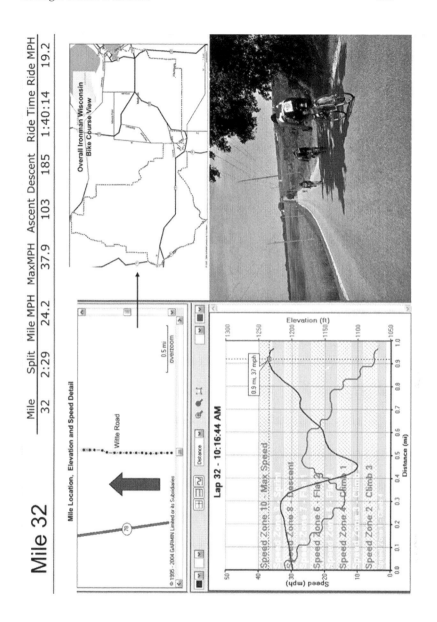

Mile 33

Mile	Split	Mile MPH	MaxMPH	Ascent	Descent	Ride Time	Ride MPH
33	3:26	17.5	37.2	120	68	1:43:40	19.1

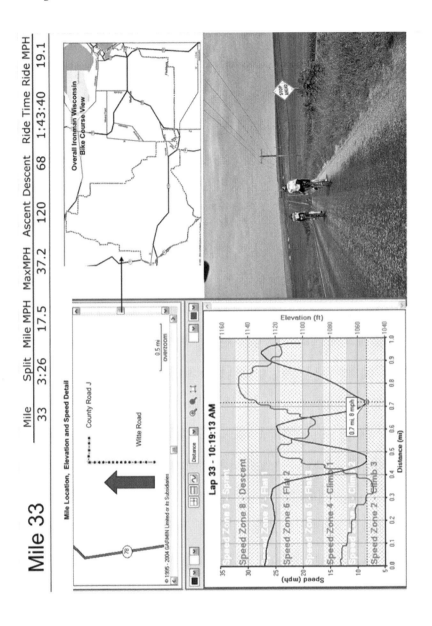

Mile 34

Mile	Split	Mile MPH	MaxMPH	Ascent	Descent	Ride Time	Ride MPH
34	3:50	15.7	32.9	122	79	1:47:30	19.0

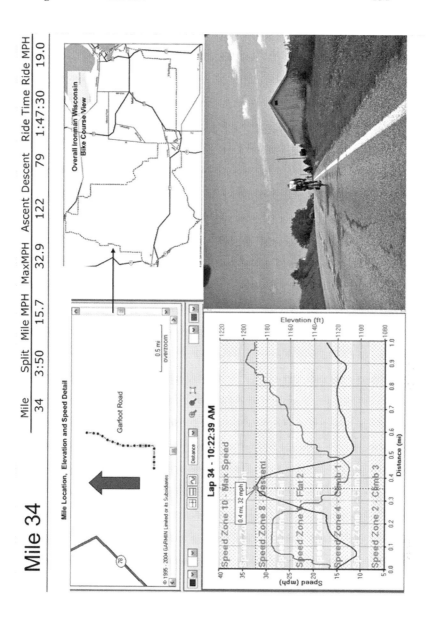

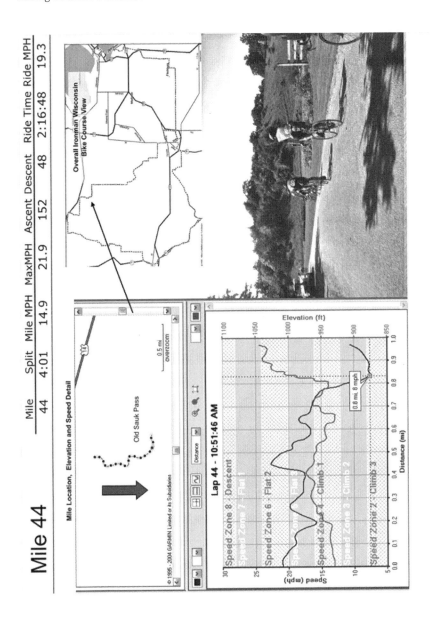

Mile	Split	Mile MPH	MaxMPH	Ascent	Descent	Ride Time	Ride MPH
44	4:01	14.9	21.9	152	48	2:16:48	19.3

Mile 44

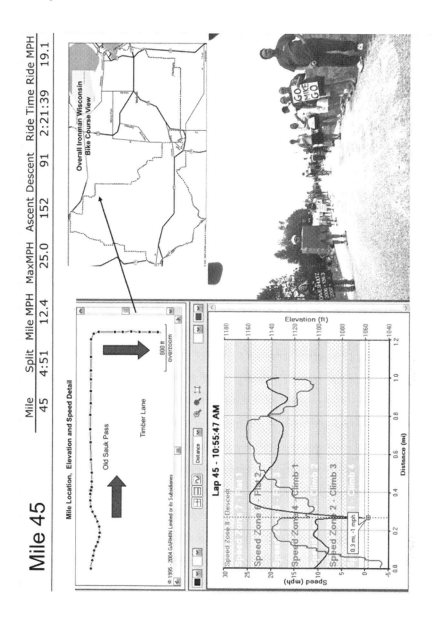

Mile	Split	Mile MPH	MaxMPH	Ascent	Descent	Ride Time	Ride MPH
45	4:51	12.4	25.0	152	91	2:21:39	19.1

Mile 46

Mile	Split	Mile MPH	MaxMPH	Ascent	Descent	Ride Time	Ride MPH
46	3:15	18.5	34.1	91	78	2:24:54	19.0

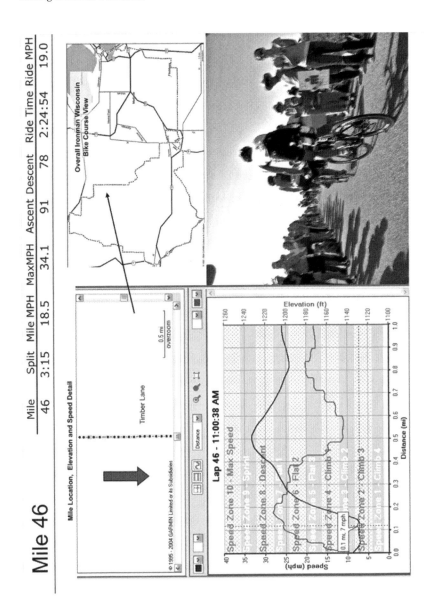

Mile	Split	Mile MPH	MaxMPH	Ascent	Descent	Ride Time	Ride MPH
54	2:54	20.7	26.2	3	79	2:46:59	19.4

Mile 54

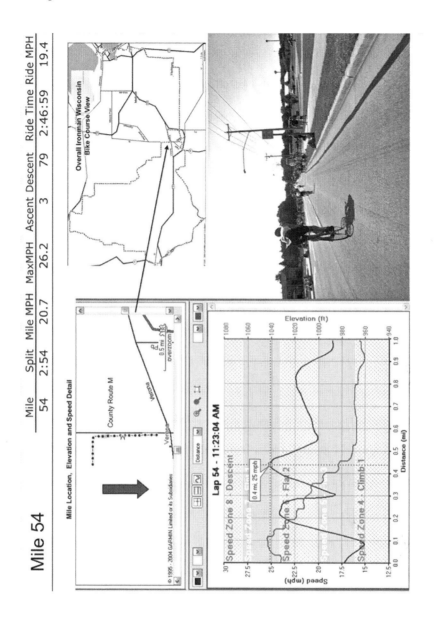

Mile	Split	Mile MPH	MaxMPH	Ascent	Descent	Ride Time	Ride MPH
86	3:11	18.8	23.4	26	21	4:28:10	19.2

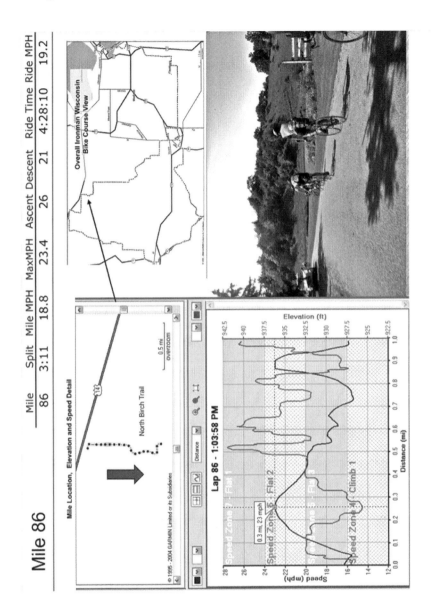

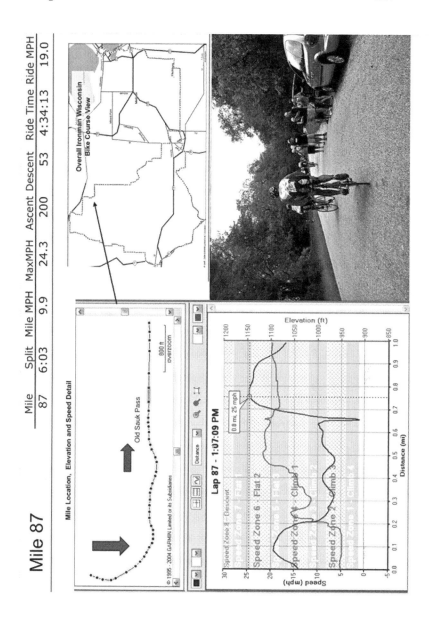

Mile	Split	Mile MPH	MaxMPH	Ascent	Descent	Ride Time	Ride MPH
87	6:03	9.9	24.3	200	53	4:34:13	19.0

Mile 87

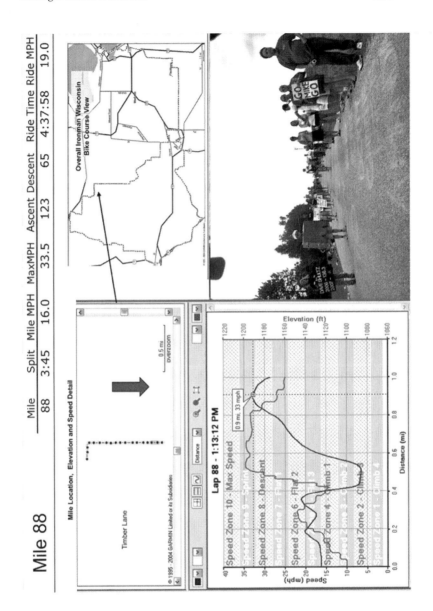

Mile	Split	Mile MPH	MaxMPH	Ascent	Descent	Ride Time	Ride MPH
89	2:30	24.0	30.0	21	17	4:40:28	19.0

Mile 89

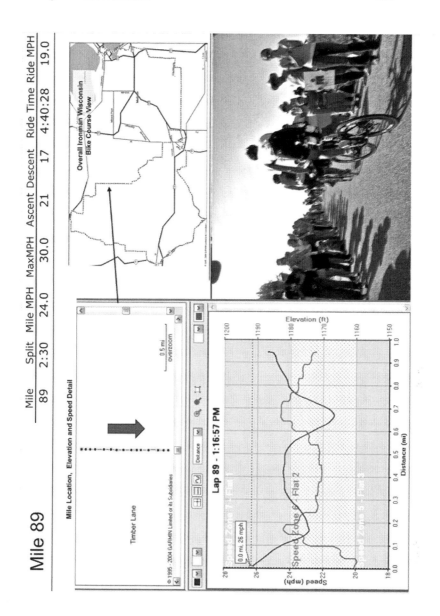

Mile 90

Mile	Split	Mile MPH	MaxMPH	Ascent	Descent	Ride Time	Ride MPH
90	2:37	22.9	32.3	57	112	4:43:05	19.1

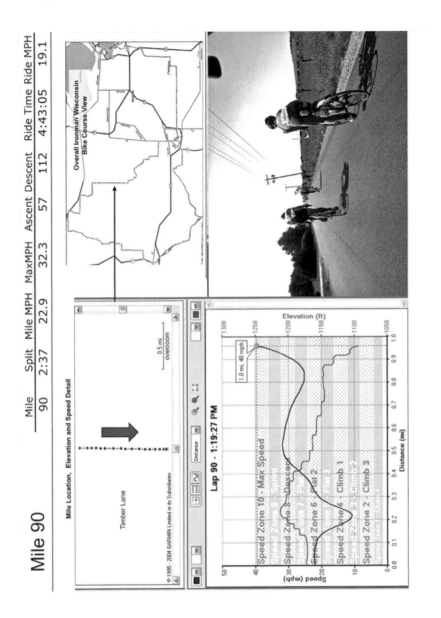

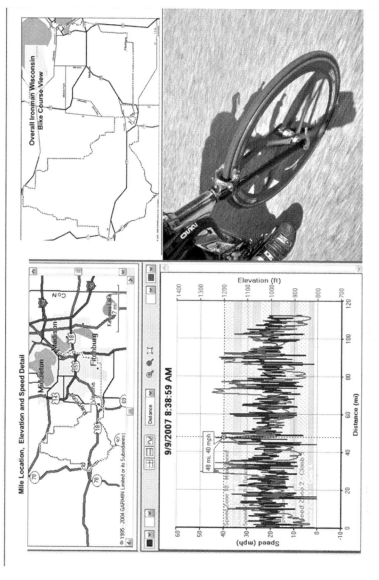

Ironman Wisconsin: Start to Finish

Ride Recap: First 56 Miles

Outbound Segment

Mile	Split	Mile MPH	MaxMPH	Ascent	Descent	Ride Time	Ride MPH
1	3:47	15.9	26.4	50	90	0:03:47	15.9
2	3:36	16.7	22.5	52	62	0:07:23	16.3
3	2:55	20.6	24.0	52	53	0:10:18	17.5
4	2:36	23.1	30.0	25	52	0:12:54	18.6
5	2:57	20.3	23.8	45	3	0:15:51	18.9
6	2:52	20.9	24.0	54	28	0:18:43	19.2
7	2:31	23.8	29.2	35	25	0:21:14	19.8
8	3:03	19.7	28.0	87	4	0:24:17	19.8
9	3:07	19.3	25.1	78	24	0:27:24	19.7
10	3:38	16.5	25.2	118	29	0:31:02	19.3
11	2:14	26.9	34.0	23	115	0:33:16	19.8
12	3:17	18.3	24.3	62	6	0:36:33	19.7
13	2:59	20.1	25.3	20	28	0:39:32	19.7
14	2:18	26.1	32.5	11	49	0:41:50	20.1
15	2:44	22.0	25.4	15	56	0:44:34	20.2
16	4:35	13.1	25.9	23	30	0:49:09	19.5

Lap 1 Segment

Mile	Split	Mile MPH	MaxMPH	Ascent	Descent	Ride Time	Ride MPH
17	5:36	10.7	32.3	68	94	0:54:45	18.6
18	3:03	19.7	37.2	111	98	0:57:48	18.7
19	2:58	20.2	29.6	46	47	1:00:46	18.8
20	2:37	22.9	25.1	17	2	1:03:23	18.9
21	3:01	19.9	25.8	55	10	1:06:24	19.0
22	3:25	17.6	26.2	100	24	1:09:49	18.9
23	2:14	26.9	33.0	25	147	1:12:03	19.2
24	2:48	21.4	29.2	42	41	1:14:51	19.2
25	3:11	18.8	23.9	57	41	1:18:02	19.2
26	2:53	20.8	31.6	95	78	1:20:55	19.3
27	3:14	18.6	24.9	118	37	1:24:09	19.3
28	3:10	18.9	21.2	63	46	1:27:19	19.2
29	4:25	13.6	20.5	148	9	1:31:44	19.0
30	3:10	18.9	25.4	51	59	1:34:54	19.0
31	2:51	21.1	26.1	35	41	1:37:45	19.0
32	2:29	24.2	37.9	103	185	1:40:14	19.2
33	3:26	17.5	37.2	120	68	1:43:40	19.1
34	3:50	15.7	32.9	122	79	1:47:30	19.0
35	3:24	17.6	28.9	89	132	1:50:54	18.9
36	2:01	29.8	36.3	26	189	1:52:55	19.1
37	2:35	23.2	30.1	42	43	1:55:30	19.2
38	2:50	21.2	26.7	38	26	1:58:20	19.3
39	2:49	21.3	27.3	28	55	2:01:09	19.3
40	2:56	20.5	23.1	35	24	2:04:05	19.3
41	2:57	20.3	23.0	66	29	2:07:02	19.4
42	2:49	21.3	27.3	18	48	2:09:51	19.4
43	2:56	20.5	24.0	23	14	2:12:47	19.4
44	4:01	14.9	21.9	152	48	2:16:48	19.3
45	4:51	12.4	25.0	152	91	2:21:39	19.1
46	3:15	18.5	34.1	91	78	2:24:54	19.0
47	2:33	23.5	28.6	40	23	2:27:27	19.1
48	1:59	30.3	44.1	28	166	2:29:26	19.3
49	3:45	16.0	33.6	153	35	2:33:11	19.2
50	3:05	19.5	40.5	71	170	2:36:16	19.2
51	2:32	23.7	40.6	78	46	2:38:48	19.3
52	2:32	23.7	31.1	28	21	2:41:20	19.3
53	2:45	21.8	27.9	26	21	2:44:05	19.3
54	2:54	20.7	26.2	3	79	2:46:59	19.4
55	3:07	19.3	21.9	13	22	2:50:06	19.4
56	2:43	22.1	25.7	55	22	2:52:49	19.4

Ride Recap: Last 56 Miles

Lap 2 Segment

Mile	Split	Mile MPH	MaxMPH	Ascent	Descent	Ride Time	Ride MPH
57	2:49	21.3	23.7	29	60	2:55:38	19.5
58	2:40	22.5	27.6	18	34	2:58:18	19.5
59	3:20	18.0	26.0	98	20	3:01:38	19.5
60	3:24	17.6	35.1	100	62	3:05:02	19.5
61	2:53	20.8	36.9	69	68	3:07:55	19.5
62	2:42	22.2	27.8	25	8	3:10:37	19.5
63	2:59	20.1	23.1	30	6	3:13:36	19.5
64	3:25	17.6	25.6	124	63	3:17:01	19.5
65	2:56	20.5	32.2	70	104	3:19:57	19.5
66	2:27	24.5	31.9	25	90	3:22:24	19.6
67	2:52	20.9	26.0	31	8	3:25:16	19.6
68	3:24	17.6	28.2	69	54	3:28:40	19.6
69	3:24	17.6	26.3	88	67	3:32:04	19.5
70	3:23	17.7	22.0	67	13	3:35:27	19.5
71	4:47	12.5	18.5	162	11	3:40:14	19.3
72	3:44	16.1	24.7	54	48	3:43:58	19.3
73	3:04	19.6	23.1	33	9	3:47:02	19.3
74	3:01	19.9	31.7	61	106	3:50:03	19.3
75	3:14	18.6	35.4	91	127	3:53:17	19.3
76	3:59	15.1	30.9	128	105	3:57:16	19.2
77	4:14	14.2	24.7	119	90	4:01:30	19.1
78	2:21	25.5	35.5	11	269	4:03:51	19.2
79	2:38	22.8	29.7	33	91	4:06:29	19.2
80	2:55	20.6	23.9	10	40	4:09:24	19.2
81	3:14	18.6	24.4	41	50	4:12:38	19.2
82	3:04	19.6	22.6	34	9	4:15:42	19.2
83	3:17	18.3	21.8	54	9	4:18:59	19.2
84	2:56	20.5	25.4	18	44	4:21:55	19.2
85	3:04	19.6	23.8	25	14	4:24:59	19.2
86	3:11	18.8	23.4	26	21	4:28:10	19.2
87	6:03	9.9	24.3	200	53	4:34:13	19.0
88	3:45	16.0	33.5	123	65	4:37:58	19.0
89	2:30	24.0	30.0	21	17	4:40:28	19.0
90	2:37	22.9	32.3	57	112	4:43:05	19.1
91	2:24	25.0	41.2	40	81	4:45:29	19.1
92	5:15	11.4	22.4	190	6	4:50:44	19.0
93	2:43	22.1	39.8	53	133	4:52:59	19.0
94	2:43	22.1	29.8	44	32	4:55:42	19.1
95	2:41	22.4	27.8	38	67	4:58:23	19.1
96	2:54	20.7	26.1	23	66	5:01:17	19.1

Inbound Segment

Mile	Split	Mile MPH	MaxMPH	Ascent	Descent	Ride Time	Ride MPH
97	3:05	19.5	21.9	7	30	5:04:22	19.1
98	2:47	21.6	23.9	3	17	5:07:09	19.1
99	3:49	15.7	21.0	131	20	5:10:58	19.1
100	3:30	17.1	26.6	62	59	5:14:28	19.1
101	2:54	20.7	29.7	14	75	5:17:22	19.1
102	3:07	19.3	26.9	45	16	5:20:29	19.1
103	3:56	15.3	32.5	106	108	5:24:25	19.0
104	2:39	22.6	28.7	27	64	5:27:04	19.1
105	2:32	23.7	29.9	17	104	5:29:36	19.1
106	3:10	18.9	28.5	74	65	5:32:46	19.1
107	3:23	17.7	20.5	18	50	5:36:09	19.1
108	2:53	20.8	26.3	18	50	5:39:02	19.1
109	3:07	19.3	21.6	52	33	5:42:09	19.1
110	3:35	16.7	23.9	48	68	5:45:44	19.1
111	3:30	17.1	21.2	25	44	5:49:14	19.1
112	2:58	20.2	21.5	38	14	5:52:12	19.1
Helix	1:45	13.0	16.0	47	32	5:53:57	19.1

Everything Else You Need To Know

At each Ironman race these days – or Half Ironman, Olympic Distance, or even Sprint races for that matter – hundreds or more of the athletes are tackling triathlon for the first time.

And they all have the same questions: What do I need to take? What do I do when I get there? What should I expect? What do I need to carry? What might go wrong? How do I deal with it?

It can seem overwhelming. So much to do, so much to remember. Let me simplify it for you.

Do what you or your coach think is right to get you to the point where you're ready to race, ready to cover the distance. I'll help you with the rest from packing for your trip to crossing the finish line:

• What to Take
• Assembly Once You Get There
• Bike Check-in
• Planning Nutrition
• Race Morning – Final Preparations
• The Race: Swim, Transition, Bike, Transition, Run
• Finishing With a Smile

It takes a few races to get it all figured out, believe me. With 29 Ironman finishes over the last nine years, I think I can pretty well answer many of those questions for rookies, and even for those that have done more than one race, but are still looking for the right combination.

What to Take

There are so many things to pack or, put another way, so many things to potentially forget. And yes, I have forgotten many different things over the years.

But I have learned not to panic, for a simple reason: even if you forgot everything, you still could buy just about all of it
 at the race merchandise area. Just knowing you have that backstop should make your packing less worrisome.

Because I'll tell you right now: you will forget something, probably a few somethings. Don't worry. Wetsuits, Bikes, components, nutrition, just about everything but running shoes (which you can buy at a sporting goods store) can typically be found on site.

But to remember to bring the right things, here's the approach: pre-pack your transition bags.

Create five piles in the packing room, one each for Prerace, Swim, Bike, Run, Nutrition. As you grab items from your closet, bags, car, wherever, lay them in the appropriate piles.

My basics are:
- Prerace: clothes to wear to/from transition – jacket and sweatpants, and what I'll wear during the entire race – bike shirt, tri-shorts, timing chip and strap
- Swim: wetsuit, goggles, sunscreen, body glide, extra swim cap, swimsuit
- Bike: helmet, sunglasses, bike shoes, gloves, race belt, socks, arm warmers
- Run: hat, shoes, extra race belt, socks, and sunglasses if you need them
- Nutrition/other: bring the essentials you are sure you won't find on the race site. A favorite gel, certain salt tablets or pain reliever, perhaps. Have a small plastic container – I prefer a 35mm film holder – to hold salt and ibuprofen on the bike.

Place the contents into five bags, labeled accordingly, and drop them in your suitcase. For me, one of those bags is an athletic bag, which I later use to carry things to/from transition.

Packing the bike can be intimidating. After dialing in your perfect position, the last thing you want to do is disassemble it. To restore your bike to that perfect position later, use black electrical tape to mark measurements. Seat post, handlebars, anything that moves or is removed should have a tape mark. Do that, and you can return to your perfect dialed-in position when you reassemble your bike.

So you're not scrambling on race day, pack your saddle bag in advance with everything you'll need before the trip. Replacement tube or tire, glue if necessary, co2 adapter (buy co2 on site), disc wheel air adapter (if necessary), hex tool, extra contact lenses (yes, you might need them).

Pressing bike pieces inside a tight transport case is a scary concept. To avoid friction in transit, wrap the frame and anything else that might have contact in bubble wrap or some other protective material. I use several Velcro straps use to secure the protection in place. And knowing how bike

cases can be tossed around behind airline counters, I've added Velcro on the outside of the case itself to further secure the contents.

Follow these steps, and you should have just about everything you need with you when you arrive at the race registration.

Assembly

Unpack soon after arriving to make sure you brought everything, or more important, to find out if you forgot anything. Time flies surprisingly fast once you get to the race city, and if you need something – I usually do, CO2 cartridges and GU at a minimum – you need to find out early.

It's especially important to get your bike assembled and tested right away. If a screw gets stripped or a tire won't inflate, you want to know that as soon as possible. There's nothing worse than finding out your bike stem needs to be replaced right before bike check-in, and then scrambling to find the right size, shape, whatever. Yes, it's happened to me, and yes, I've panicked when the right part couldn't be found. You don't want that to happen to you.

After you get your race transition bags at registration, lay them out, and match the Swim, Bike, Run bags you had packed earlier. It's as simple as transferring the contents – you've already pre-packed your transition bags. Again, if you forgot anything, you'll find out at this time, and have the opportunity to buy what's missing.

An important note about bib numbers and race belts. Bib numbers can be flimsy, can tear, and can fly off during the race. And losing your number can mean a penalty (silly rule, but I've seen it enforced). My secret to avoiding all this: black electrical tape. Put black electrical tape over the top two holes of your bib number, front and back. This more than doubles the reinforcement. Then poke the pin on your race belt through the electrical tape to secure the bib number. The electrical tape holds perfectly. I've never lost a bib number on the course with this method.

Bike Check-In

In my early races, I remember being particularly worried that I'd forgotten something essential on the day of bike and transition bag check-in the day before the race. I'd check and recheck the bags, and still be nervous.

But there's no reason for concern. At most races, you have access to your bags race morning, and if you forget anything, you can add it then. Again, relax.

Just make sure you've got the basics in the bags: bib number, helmet, bike shoes, running shoes. If you swim in your tri-outfit, you can finish the race with just those items. Everything else – sunglasses, gloves, socks, hat – extra. If you have it there, perfect. If you forgot, don't sweat it.

It's pretty easy to find bikes belonging to some of the triathlon rookies at any race. How to spot them? Easy. Three water bottles already in cages on the bike, and nutrition already put in place. PowerBar squares sticking to the top tube of some bikes, an open invitation for bugs. Nasty.

Believe me, after exposure to a hot day and a cool night, that stuff will not be appealing on race day. Keep your nutrition and bottles with you overnight, and put them in place on race morning.

I had a string of triathlons that involved rain the night before the race, and now bring plastic trash bags to put over handlebars and the seat if the forecast suggests a wet night. Covering the handlebars means a dry surface to tape nutrition (all my GU slipped off wet handlebars in transition at one race). Some people cover their chain, too. Some cover the entire bike. That's overkill for me, but it's up to you.

After that, you'll have nothing to do except relax and think about the nutrition and hydration you'll carry the following day.

Planning Race Nutrition

Planning your hydration and nutrition needs for an Ironman can be tricky. Too much and you'll feel sick, too little and you'll bonk. And then there's the worry about how to get enough calories during the day. I've seen sandwiches strapped to handlebars. I've ridden with riders whose watches beeped every fifteen minutes telling them to eat more fig bars. I've seen athletes load up a Camelback to carry fluid with them on the bike and the same athletes stop in their tracks at Special Needs to reload another bladder of fluid.

It all seems like so much work. It has to be simpler.

It took me many races of trial and error to find the right mix. What I ended up with may be a formula that can be applied to your needs, though the specific ingredients might change.

After many races, I found that about 2500 to 3000 calories was my optimal calorie count on the bike. Simply, that translates to about 250 calories every 10 miles on the bike. This amount not only keeps me fueled for the bike, but also prepares me for the run. So that is my target. Practice caloric intake on your long training rides to find the level right for you.

In terms of how to get those calories, here's what I came up with:

- 800 calories GU: 8 packets, 100 calories each, Plain is the preferred flavor
- 920 calories PowerBars: 4 chocolate PowerBars,
- 300 calories: Bananas: grab 6 bananas at aid stations
- 750 calories Gatorade: take at least 5 bottles Gatorade, one every other aid station, 5 x 125 calories

Race Morning: Final Preparations

My race morning routine is simple.

First, you can arrive terrifyingly early. Don't. As long as you can get there an hour before the race, you're fine. Arrive two hours early, and you've added anxiety time. Relax.

Second, get the bike ready:

- Tape the 8 GU gels to aerobars, four on each side
- Place four PowerBars in Profile-Design Velcro pouch on the top of my Softride beam
- Put the plastic container (35mm film) container with ibuprofen and sodium in the pouch
- Insert one water bottle in bottle cage (with regular aid stations, I see no reason to carry more)
- Check the tires
- Put White Lightning on the chain
- Set the bike computer distance and time setting to zero

Next, I go to transition area and make sure at least helmet, bike shoes, bib number and running shoes are in the bags. That's the minimum you need, if you forgot anything.

After that. Relax, breathe deep, and look forward to a fun day of endurance. Now all you have to do is travel 140.6 miles (or the distance of your triathlon). Again, don't worry. Plenty of time -- you've got 17 hours to do it.

Swim

In my experience, not too much can go terribly wrong in the swim. You get through it, either quickly, or not. How fast you go depends on your training.

How much physical contact you endure depends on where you start. I've tried starting everywhere: at the rear, up front, inside on the 'line', outside. There will be contact no matter where you start.

Someone will inadvertently kick you. You will accidentally bump into someone else. It may feel violent, but no one wants to hurt anyone. Do not take it personally. Know that the person who almost knocked your goggles off really wished that didn't happen, sorry. Relax.

If you start at the rear and you're willing to wait about 30 seconds after the cannon goes off, it can be a fairly breezy swim. The benefit is a complete draft of all swimmers in front of you; the downside may be that you need to navigate around many people.

Most of the time, I hope to start on the side, near the front, with the hope that it will not be congested. Except that hundreds of athletes also seem to have the same idea. So the sides tend to be pretty densely packed.

For the rookie who's not an expert swimmer, relax at the swim start, let others start ahead of you, and do your best to swim in a straight line. If you lose five or ten minutes on a slow swim, you can make it up on the bike or run.

For the rookies who are fast swimmers, I envy you. Go to the front, swim well, and enjoy being in front of most of the athletes for a while. Say hi to me when I pass you on the bike.

Swim to Bike Transition

I am usually disoriented coming out of the water. It's not easy to immediately adjust to land after more than an hour bobbing and weaving through the water. Take your time exiting the water, and begin running to transition. Volunteers may be there to help remove your wetsuit. After that, other volunteers will help you find your transition bag. Thank them for helping you.

Find a seat, put on your helmet, bib number, socks and shoes. Make sure debris is off your feet first, because you may choose to run in those socks later. Decide if you want to take arm warmers. My advice: when in doubt, be comfortable. I usually wear arm warmers on the bike, knowing I might discard them later. And I'm usually glad I have them.

Get sunscreen before you head out to get your bike. Volunteers will slather it on you in fifteen seconds. Skip that step, and you will be explaining strange sunburn patterns to your family later.

Bike

For me, the first few hours on the bike are perhaps the most enjoyable part of the Ironman. You feel fresh, you feel fast, people are in good moods. And then there's the scenery. Every course has wonderful scenery, in its own way. It's one of the reasons we race.

Can something go wrong on your bike ride, the one you prepared so diligently for? Sure. Be prepared for it, not afraid.

Something different seems to happen to me in every race. I've had flat tires in Austria and in the US. I've had contact lenses fly out of my eyes on the bike in Canada and in Germany. More than once I've pulled my bike out of transition, only to see 1000 calories of nutrition fly off the bike onto the street (I've learned a thing or two about securing nutrition in place as a result).

The point is, expect the unexpected, and embrace it as part of the triathlon experience. Being a triathlete is about overcoming obstacles. Unexpected problems included.

I saw several people on the side of the road on the Ironman Arizona 2006 bike course with flat tires or some other bike mechanical problem. More than a few of them had looks of deep despair, head in hands. They were looks of shattered dreams. And at the moment, they may have been. But there are other chances, other races. I've done enough races to know that a single race is never the definitive one. Do what you can to get back on the course, and finish.

If you get a flat tire, try to change it. I flew all the way to Austria, in hope of a fast race in 2001, only to flat on the first loop. I lost 10 minutes changing the flat, and that wasn't too bad. I didn't let it kill my day.

In Ironman USA Lake Placid 2005, two of the three screws on my cycling shoe cleat fell out. I stropped to try to fix it to no avail, then rode the last 25 miles gingerly with a loose cleat. It cost me many precious minutes (and I missed a Kona slot by one minute), but I've decided life is too short to worry about things that happen. They do. You'll be fine.

If you need to wait for race support for help, it could take a long time. If that happens, don't get upset, just change your goal. A friend waited 45 minutes waiting for assistance at Ironman Idaho, after which he found himself almost completely at the rear of all athletes. So he changed the challenge. He would now try to see how many people he could pass for the remainder of the bike ride. He must have passed more than 1000 people, and was satisfied with that.

Executing the bike nutrition plan is about as simple as putting it together. Remember, your exact nutrition may vary, but the concept is the same – balanced calorie input throughout your ride. Here's the timing. Simple.

- GU: Take a GU sometime within every 10 mile segment. That gets you to 80 miles. Easy to remember, each time you see a mile marker with a zero, eat a GU.
- PowerBar: Eat a PowerBar within every 25 mile segment. Yes, this overlaps with GU somewhat, but that's not a problem. I usually eat them between miles 15 and 20, 40 and 45, and 65 and 70. The last one depends on how I'm feeling late in the ride.
- Gatorade: it's essential to always have one with you on the bike. Grab one each aid station and put it in a bottle cage.
- Water: I also grab a water bottle, but try to swig half of it then toss it by the end of the aid station. With aid stations every 10 miles, I can't come up with a reason to carry more than one bottle.
- Bananas: it's unpredictable which aid stations will have them, so I grab one each time I see it. Some races do not have bananas, and you might have to substitute. Just make sure you grab those 300 calories somewhere.
- Salt/Ibuprofen: I took a salt tablet and an ibuprofen tablet every 30 miles. Read directions to make sure your ibuprofen dose is appropriate.

I don't use special needs bags on the bike or run. I decided long ago it's not worth the hassle. Everything I need is on the bike or at aid stations. I think the same is true for most athletes. Not to mention my experience is that getting your bag in a timely manner tends to be a challenge, and most of the time what you included in the bag is not appealing when you actually get it.

Bike To Run Transition

By the time you finish the bike, you're feeling ready to run. At least mentally. Ready to run in the sense that you're ready to not ride anymore, at a minimum.

Reality will set in when you hop off the bike, give it to a waiting volunteer, and begin to head towards transition. Those first few steps after 112 miles are quite a surprise. You feel like you almost can't move forward. Your first thought may be: I don't think I can 26.2 miles now.

Rest assured that in about 30 seconds, you'll feel better. Keep running, pick up your bag, and get to the change tent. By the time you get your running shoes and hat on, you'll feel surprisingly ready to run. Get more sunscreen, acknowledge the cheers of the spectators on the railing, and head out onto the run course.

Run

In the same way you might get a flat tire on the run, you may physically flat on the run. Cramps, bad patches, tough times. For the Ironman rookie, this might be the longest continuous timeframe you've ever moved your body forward. It may want to give out soon. But know that sometimes it can get better after it gets worse. Keep moving forward, keep hydrating and drinking.

Most aid stations, usually only one mile apart, have water, cola, Gatorade, chicken broth, oranges, bananas, pretzels, GU and ice. Train with these, and you'll need nothing more on race day.

The run hydration/nutrition plan is even simpler than on the bike, because you don't need to carry anything. I've worked out similar 'rules' for consistency, including:

- Two cups of cola with ice at least every other aid station. Cola provides sugar, caffeine and sodium. That's about 50 calories x 13 = 650 calories
- If bearable, GU every 4 miles. That's about 600 calories if you get them all.
- When the chicken broth is available, take it. It's Go Juice. High levels of sodium will make you feel better, guaranteed. Though the mix of cola and broth in your stomach might not feel the best.

At Ironman Arizona, because of the very dry air, I found myself needing to have cola at every aid station. Do what you need to do. The only thing to avoid is getting behind on your hydration or nutrition. Try to keep up.

And run as the best you can, at least at a pace that you can sustain for a few hours. If you need to walk a hill or two, do it. Walk the aid stations. Keep moving forward. Nothing will keep you from your Ironman finish. It's just a matter of time now.

Finish

You've trained all year to get there. You've raced all day to get there. Enjoy the moments in the final meters of the finish line chute. Let others enjoy their moment, too. Don't race someone to the finish line, unless you think a Kona slot is on the line. Let the racer in front of you get a finish line photo to cherish. Then go get your own.

Cross the line, smile for the camera, and consider yourself a member of the club. You are an Ironman.

Finish Line

I hope this Book provides the information you need to have a great Ironman race. If there are some questions that still need answers, feel free to contact me via my website, www.RunTri.com.

There is no experience like racing and finishing the Ironman Triathlon. But the experience getting there can be every bit as rewarding, too.

Good luck in your quest for your best Ironman race. There is no experience like racing and finishing the Ironman Triathlon. But the experience getting there can be every bit as rewarding, too. Enjoy every minute.

About the Author

Raymond Britt is Managing Partner at WinSight Ventures, publisher of RunTri.com and one of the most experienced endurance athletes in the world.

Few can match Britt's extensive competitive record. He's completed 29 Ironman Triathlons (2.4 mile swim, 112 mile bike ride, 26.2 mile run), 48 Marathons, 8 Ultramarathons (31 or more miles) and more than 60 other triathlons and running races.

Since his debut race – the 1994 Chicago Marathon – Britt has covered nearly 50,000 training and racing miles around the globe. He's finished the Chicago Marathon 12 times, the Boston Marathon 13 consecutive times, Hawaii Ironman World Championships 3 times, and has been a USA Triathlon All-American.

Britt's articles, photographs and perspectives have been featured by CNN, NBC, New York Times, USA Today, Chicago Tribune, Chicago Sun-Times, Los Angeles Times, Triathlete magazine, Running Times magazine and many others.

As publisher of RunTri.com, Britt serves an annual audience of 500,000 worldwide readers, providing free training and racing resources to help athletes achieve their goals.

Made in the USA
Lexington, KY
31 January 2015